## JUMPING FROGS
Undiscovered, Rediscovered, and Celebrated Writings of Mark Twain

NAMED AFTER ONE OF MARK TWAIN'S BEST-KNOWN AND MOST
BELOVED SHORT STORIES, THE JUMPING FROGS SERIES OF BOOKS BRINGS
NEGLECTED TREASURES FROM MARK TWAIN'S PEN TO READERS.

Mark Twain's Helpful Hints for Good Living

# Mark Twain's Helpful Hints for Good Living

## A HANDBOOK FOR THE DAMNED HUMAN RACE

Edited by Lin Salamo, Victor Fischer,
and Michael B. Frank of the Mark Twain Project

THE MARK TWAIN PROJECT IS A RESEARCH AND EDITORIAL PROJECT
HOUSED WITHIN THE MARK TWAIN PAPERS AT THE BANCROFT LIBRARY,
UNIVERSITY OF CALIFORNIA, BERKELEY.

UNIVERSITY OF CALIFORNIA PRESS
Berkeley    Los Angeles    London

*Frontispiece: Mark Twain, September 1908.*
*Photograph by Isabel V. Lyon.*

UNIVERSITY OF CALIFORNIA PRESS
Berkeley and Los Angeles, California
University of California Press, Ltd.
London, England

Library of Congress Cataloging-in-Publication Data

Twain, Mark, 1835–1910.
Mark Twain's helpful hints for good living : a handbook for the
damned human race / Mark Twain ; edited by Lin Salamo, Victor Fischer,
and Michael B. Frank of the Mark Twain Project
p.   cm.—(Jumping frogs ; 2)
Includes bibliographical references.
ISBN 0-520-24245-9 (cloth : alk. paper)
1. Conduct of life—Quotations, maxims, etc.   2. Conduct of life—
Literary collections.   3. Twain, Mark, 1835–1910—Quotations.
I. Salamo, Lin.   II. Fischer, Victor, 1942–   III. Frank, Michael B.
IV. Bancroft Library. Mark Twain Project.   V. Title.
PS1303.S25   2004
818'.409—dc22   2003024224

Manufactured in the United States of America
13   12   11   10   09   08   07   06   05   04
10   9   8   7   6   5   4   3   2   1
The paper used in this publication meets the minimum requirements
of ANSI/NISO Z39.48–1992 (R 1997) *(Permanence of Paper)*. ♾

*The human race consists of the
damned and the ought-to-be damned.*

—

*Good friends, good books, and a sleepy
conscience: this is the ideal life.*

FROM MARK TWAIN'S NOTEBOOK, 1900

# ❧[ Contents ]❧

# ❦ Illustrations ❦

#  Introduction

IN OCTOBER 1865, JUST SHY OF HIS THIRTIETH BIRTHDAY, SAMUEL LANGHORNE Clemens found himself scraping along in San Francisco, having attempted and abandoned a succession of careers: journeyman printer, Mississippi River steamboat pilot, miner, stock speculator, journalist. His fortunes and his spirits had been at lowest ebb but were now—after some bitter soul-searching—beginning to rebound. He wrote to his brother on 19 October:

> I never had but two **powerful** ambitions in my life. One was to be a pilot,
> & the other a preacher of the gospel. I accomplished the one & failed in the
> other, **because** I could not supply myself with the necessary stock in trade—
> *i.e.* religion. . . . But I *have* had a "call" to literature, of a low order—*i.e.*
> humorous. It is nothing to be proud of, but it is my strongest suit.

He vowed to concentrate his attention on "seriously scribbling to excite the **laughter** of God's creatures." And within four years Clemens—otherwise "Mark Twain," the pseudonym he had adopted in 1863—had transcended his local fame as an irreverent, sometimes controversial, journalist and author of occasional humorous sketches, known on the West Coast as "the Moralist of the Main."

With a commission to write for the *San Francisco Alta California*, he traveled to Europe and the Holy Land—the wild card in an organized tour of wealthy, pious Americans. The fresh and amusing travel letters of the rambunctious young "pilgrim" were avidly read across the nation as they appeared in 1867 and 1868. He honed his travel account into a full-length book, *The Innocents Abroad*, which from its publication in 1869 was a runaway best seller. Over the next forty years—in travel books, novels, sketches, lectures, and speeches—"Mark Twain" came to embody the most distinct and well-known American literary voice in the world. At the same time, his personal life as Samuel Langhorne Clemens captured the interest of the public. In 1870 he married Olivia (Livy) Langdon, the shy, well-bred daughter of a wealthy New York coal dealer; he had four children, dreamed of a peaceful, loving home life, and during a halcyon twenty-year period saw that dream largely fulfilled. But bitter losses darkened his life: he lost his son, Langdon, in infancy, in 1872; his adored oldest daughter, Susy, died suddenly of meningitis in 1896, at the age of twenty-four. He dreamed of building a fortune from business but lost everything and in 1894 suffered the public humiliation of bankruptcy. Forced by financial need to travel around the world in 1895–96 on a lecture tour, he was greeted as a much-loved friend by audiences as far from home as Australia and India. He used the proceeds from the tour to pay back his creditors and with the help of a new friend—Henry H. Rogers, vice president of Standard Oil—recouped his fortunes. He lost his beloved Olivia in 1904 and his youngest daughter, Jean, a few months before his own death in April 1910.

Late in his life, as his good friend William Dean Howells recalled in *My Mark Twain* (1910), Clemens began "to amass those evidences against mankind which eventuated with him in his theory of what he called 'the damned human race'":

> This was not an expression of piety, but of the kind of contempt to which he
> was driven by our follies and iniquities as he had observed them in himself as
> well as in others. It was as mild a misanthropy, probably, as ever caressed the
> objects of its malediction. But I believe it was about the year 1900 that his sense
> of our perdition became insupportable and broke out in a mixed abhorrence

and amusement which spared no occasion, so that I could quite understand why Mrs. Clemens should have found some compensation, when kept to her room by sickness, in the reflection that now she should not hear so much about "the damned human race." . . . Nothing came of his pose regarding "the damned human race" except his invention of the Human Race Luncheon Club. This was confined to four persons [Clemens, Howells, the humorist Finley P. Dunne, and the president of Harper and Brothers, George B. Harvey] who were never all got together, and it soon perished of their indifference.

Howells's assertion that "nothing came" of Clemens's investigations into the "follies and iniquities" of "the damned human race" is myopic: they fueled his late writing and drove his independent and outspoken social and political criticism.

In his last years Clemens held court wherever he went—much admired and lionized and respected. He had called on humor to prick the bubble of pretension and mindless convention, to assail corruption and injustice, and had delighted us with abundant invention. He amply fulfilled his calling of "scribbling to excite the **laughter** of God's creatures," and along the way he also realized that other dream and became—if not a "preacher of the gospel"—a "moralist in disguise," as he admitted in 1902.

————————

THIS COLLECTION brings together, under eight broad headings, some of Mark Twain's thoughts on family life, private and public manners, ethics, and personal style, as selected by the editors of the Mark Twain Project at the University of California in Berkeley. Together the selections constitute an idiosyncratic guide through the choppy waters of daily life, a sort of eccentric etiquette for the human race, pieced together from anecdotes, whimsical suggestions, maxims, and cautionary tales. His ruminations on the stages of one's moral education and on civil behavior within the home circle as well as abroad; his opinions about dress, health, food, and child rearing; and his suggestions on subjects ranging from how to deal with burglars to how to gain admittance into heaven are scattered throughout his writings, both private and published, sometimes elaborated in essays and speeches, sometimes captured in a few axiomatic words. He exercised his impulse to instruct as well as amuse, sometimes using the straightforward form of autobiographical memoir (see, for example, "On Theft and Conscience" and "Youthful Misdemeanors" in this collection), at other times disguising his lessons as skewed moral tales (some comic, some dark) or as burlesques of Sunday school literature, temperance tracts, and etiquette manuals (see "At the Funeral").

Some of the texts included here are complete; some are excerpted from longer works. Some selections are culled from Clemens's personal letters, autobiographical writings, and speeches; some are from his novels and sketches. The latter sometimes turn out to be autobiographical after all, for Clemens's real life was often transformed into Mark Twain's fiction. "I have . . . been forced by fate to adopt fiction as a medium of truth," Clemens said in 1900. "Most liars lie for the love of the lie; I lie for the love of truth. I disseminate my true views by means of a series of apparently humorous and mendacious stories." The dinner of turnips and water immortalized in *The Gilded Age* (see "A Remarkable Dinner") turns out to have been suffered through by Clemens himself at the home of an improvident relative. Sam and Livy, neophyte homeowners and new parents, are the "McWilliamses" (see "Experience of the McWilliamses with Membranous Croup"), whose household travails were captured in three humorous sketches between 1875 and 1882. Clemens's actual travel experiences are the meat and potatoes of *The Innocents Abroad* (1869), *Roughing It* (1872), *A Tramp Abroad* (1880), and *Following the Equator* (1897), even though they are served up by Mark Twain with a distinctive gravy of comical exaggeration and irony. Some of the family anecdotes and character sketches treated lightly and humorously in speeches and autobiographical writings turn up again in the darker fictions that Mark Twain wrote—and left unfinished—in the late 1890s. He often reworked and transformed his experiences for different literary purposes. Thus, in a letter of January 1879 to his friend Joseph Hopkins Twichell, Clemens told of his fumbling hunt for a lost sock in a Munich hotel room, during which he woke his sleeping wife. In his notebook, he drafted a new version of the story, relocated it to Heilbronn, and made Twichell his companion; he later expanded the draft into chapter 13 of *A Tramp Abroad*, with a fictional companion, Harris, taking the place of Twichell (see "A Night Excursion in a Hotel Room"). Finally, he retold the ostensibly truthful anecdote, again set in Heilbronn with Twichell as his companion, in a speech of March 1906.

Clemens had a simple, conventional vision of the good life, centered about a tranquil domestic circle, which he articulated for his bride-to-be in a letter of 27 February 1869:

> I have such visions every day of my life, now. And they always take one favorite shape—peace, & quiet—rest, & seclusion from the rush & roar & discord of the world—You & I apart from the jangling elements of the outside world, reading & studying together when the day's duties are done—in our own castle, by our own fireside, blessed in each other's unwavering love & confidence. But it makes me ever so restive, Livy!—& impatient to throw off these wandering duties that thrall me now, & take you to my arms, never to miss your dear presence again. Speed the day!

Eventually the household—and Clemens's vision—expanded to include three daughters. For their education and amusement, he invented games and serial stories; he joined them in amateur theatricals and fondly kept a manuscript record of their small troubles and childish sayings (excerpted here as "A Sampling of Childish Ethics").

Inevitably, domestic tranquillity was challenged by Clemens's engagement in business and current affairs and by the imperatives of his literary life—unfettered time being a basic requirement for a writer. But despite a hectic schedule of writing, lecturing, and business demands, he took a great interest in household affairs. Like all homeowners, he had to deal with community issues (see "Proposal Regarding Local Flooding" and "About the Proposed Street-Widening") and with importunate salesmen ("Political Economy" and "An Unwanted Magazine Subscription"), capricious utilities and appliances ("Complaint about Unreliable Service"), the fitful burglar alarm ("Burglary and the Well-Tempered Householder"), and the erratic telephone ("A Christmas Wish" and "On Telephones and Swearing"). He fussed over purchases of furnaces, fire screens, and music boxes; he fiddled with labor-saving inventions like his adjustable garment strap and his improved bed clamp; and he intervened in the domestic dramas of the servants' quarters. He consulted with plumbers and endured the discomforts of renovation: "We are in our carpetless & dismantled home," he wrote to friends in 1881, "living like a gang of tramps on the second floor, the rest of the house in the hands of mechanics & decorators. We have pulled down the kitchen & rebuilt it, adding twenty feet to it, & have lowered the ground in front of the greenhouse, & also carried the driveway a hundred feet further to the east (downtownwards) before it enters the Avenue. Excellent improvements."

Along with these practical matters, he provided the ultimate refinement of his vision of domestic bliss: he made sure his homes were always well supplied with cats. "Next to a wife whom I idolise, give me [a] cat—an *old* cat, with kittens," he wrote to Olivia in 1873. Decades later he was just as convinced of this fundamental principle, noting in *Pudd'nhead Wilson:* "A home without a cat—and a well-fed, well-petted and properly revered cat—may be a perfect home, perhaps, but how can it prove title?"

In the library of their house in Hartford, Connecticut, the Clemenses added a brass plate to the fireplace, inscribed, "The ornament of a house is the friends who frequent it." Over the years, in that house and in rented villas and town homes, and finally in the last house Clemens built for himself, Stormfield in Redding, Connecticut, friends and family came as houseguests and dinner guests, for billiards and cigars, for literary collaborations, for amateur theatricals, poetry clubs, and musical evenings. He was a generous host and, with the help of his wife and daughters, an attentive dinner companion (see "An Innovative Dinner Party Signal System"). Still, as Howells recalled in *My Mark Twain*, "in moments of intense excitement," he was apt to jump up from the dinner table and "walk up and down the room, flying his napkin and talking and talking." Dinners at the Clemens home, under the watchful eye of Olivia Clemens, were elaborate and elegant. In 1925 the Clemenses' longtime servant, Katy Leary, described in her memoir (*A Lifetime with Mark Twain*, written by Mary Lawton) "the most beautiful dinners that I ever heard of before or since":

> We had soup first, of course, and then the beef or ducks, you know, and then we'd have wine with our cigars, and we'd have sherry, claret, and champagne, maybe— Now what else? Oh, yes! We'd always have crème de menthe and most always charlotte russe, too. Then we'd sometimes have Nesselrode pudding and very often ice cream for the most elegant dinners. No, never plain ordinary ice cream—we always had our ice cream put up in some wonderful shapes—like flowers or cherubs, little angels—all different kinds and different shapes and flavors, and colors—oh! everything lovely!

Clemens's own culinary sensibilities did not require such elegance, but he did have a deep and sensuous appreciation of American food, particularly the simple homegrown southern dishes of his youth (see "Memories of Food on an American Farm" and "American versus European Food").

Clemens did not hesitate to share his eccentric health notions (see "Smoking, Diet, and Health at Age Seventy"). As Howells remembered:

He was apt, for a man who had put faith so decidedly away from him, to take it back and pin it to some superstition, usually of a hygienic sort. Once, when he was well on in years, he came to New York without glasses, and announced that he and all his family, so astigmatic and myopic and old-sighted, had, so to speak, burned their spectacles behind them upon the instruction of some sage who had found out that they were a delusion. The next time he came he wore spectacles freely, almost ostentatiously, and I heard from others that the whole Clemens family had been near losing their eyesight by the miracle worked in their behalf.

Periodically he would become enthused about a new health or diet regime (see "A Healthful Cocktail"), usually quirky. "Sometimes," Katy Leary remembered, "he would just leave off eating everything except one thing, and would live on that all the time. Then there was a certain kind of bread he would have to have; and he took it into his head once to live just on breakfast food, and ran all about with it. Why, he would even go to dinners and parties and carry that old breakfast food with him!"

He had firm views about what constituted comfortable and eye-catching attire (see "That White Suit," "Clothes and Deception," and "A Sumptuous Robe"). In his own way, he was as much a man of style—distinctive in both dress and manner—as his contemporaries Whistler and Wilde. When she met Clemens for the first time in 1872, Lilian Aldrich, the very proper wife of the writer and editor Thomas Bailey Aldrich, was shocked by his appearance and by his curious hesitating drawl, which she mistook for inebriation. In her *Crowding Memories* (1920), she wrote:

> Mr. Aldrich came home bringing with him a most unusual guest, clothed in a coat of sealskin, the fur worn outward; a sealskin cap well down over his ears; the cap half revealing and half concealing the mass of reddish hair underneath; the heavy mustache having the same red tint. The trousers

came well below the coat, and were of a yellowish-brown color; stockings of the same tawny hue, which the low black shoe emphasized. May and December intermixed, producing strange confusion in one's preconceived ideas. Was it the dress for winter, or was it the dress for summer? Seemingly it all depended on the range of vision. If one looked up, winter; if one looked down, summer. But when the wearer spoke it was not difficult for the listener to believe that he was not entirely accountable for the strange gear. It was but too evident that he had looked upon the cup when it was red, for seemingly it had both cheered and inebriated, as the gentleman showed marked inability to stand perpendicular, but swayed from side to side, and had also difficulty with his speech; he did not stammer exactly, but after each word he placed a period. . . . Winter disappeared with the removal of the guest's fur coat and cap, and summer, or at least early springtime, emerged in the violet tint of the carelessly tied neck-knot, and the light gray of under coat and waistcoat.

Mark Twain's knack for the pithy remark is evident in all his writing, both early and late. For instance, in his 1866 notebook we find, "Rise early—it is the early bird that catches the worm. Don't be fooled by this absurd saw. I once knew a man who tried it. He got up at sunrise & a horse bit him." And the notebooks he kept after 1900 contain numerous drafts of new maxims. In 1894 Mark Twain used aphorisms—supposed to be part of a "whimsical almanac" seasoned with "a little dab of ostensible philosophy, usually in ironical form"— to introduce the chapters in *The Tragedy of Pudd'nhead Wilson*. The sayings were then gathered into a tiny (about two-by-three-inch) booklet, which was distributed along with the installments of the novel serialized in the *Century Magazine*. Pudd'nhead Wilson's maxims proved so popular that Mark Twain created a second series for *Following the Equator* in 1897. In tone and intention, Mark Twain's maxims are perhaps more akin to the brisk practicalities spoken by Benjamin Franklin's Poor Richard Saunders than the sour witticisms of Ambrose Bierce. Now and again, however, Mark Twain used the form to express succinctly an underlying cynicism and disillusionment. As he noted in 1902, "The man who is a pessimist before 48, knows too much; if he is an optimist after it, he knows too little."

---

THIS COLLECTION has been prepared by the staff at the Mark Twain Papers, which is part of the special collections of The Bancroft Library at the University of California in Berkeley. Within this renowned archive, for almost forty years, the Mark Twain Project has been researching, editing, and publishing both scholarly and popular editions of the author's literary works and private papers. In our narrow suite of offices, hedged in by manuscripts and original documents, clippings, photographs, reference works, and stacks of proofs, we welcome visiting scholars and continue to produce new volumes (already numbering nearly forty). Most of the small staff of editors has been here for thirty or more years, yet Mark Twain's work still provokes and animates us: political and social issues, language and literary style are debated; one still hears the sudden splutter of laughter as a work is proofread.

The pieces we have selected we have all read many times, and they continue to delight us. Mark Twain is always a welcome companion—clear-eyed, humorous, occasionally cantankerous, never afraid of a forceful expression or a cathartic outburst. We invite you to enjoy these glimpses of Mark Twain's philosophy of living and hope they will incite you to seek out others.

LIN SALAMO

# Mark Twain's Helpful Hints for Good Living

No. 1

Shall

I learn to
be good
. . . . . .
. . . . . .
I will sit
here and
think it
over.

Truly Yours

Mark Twain

Sept.
'06

#  Everyday Etiquette

Daily life is full of baffling social obligations and
small annoyances, which require restraint as well as
tact and courtesy.

→ The highest perfection of politeness
   is only a beautiful edifice, built, from the
   base to the dome, of graceful and gilded
   forms of charitable and unselfish lying.

→ Etiquette requires us to admire the
   human race.

# A Letter of Apology

(1876)

Hartford June 14/76.

I am a long time answering your letter, my dear Miss Harriet, but then you must remember that it is an equally long time since I received it—so that makes us even, & nobody to blame on either side. . . .

Truly Yrs

S. L. Clemens. Mark Twain

# About the Effect of Intemperate Language

(from a 1906 autobiographical dictation)

All through the first ten years of my married life I kept a constant and discreet watch upon my tongue while in the house, and went outside and to a distance when circumstances were too much for me and I was obliged to seek relief. I prized my wife's respect and approval above all the rest of the human race's respect and approval. I dreaded the day when she should discover that I was but a whited sepulchre partly freighted with suppressed language. I was so careful, during ten years, that I had not a doubt that my suppressions had been successful. Therefore I was quite as happy in my guilt as I could have been if I had been innocent.

But at last an accident exposed me. I went into the bath-room one morning to make my toilet, and carelessly left the door two or three inches ajar. It was the first time that I had ever failed to take the precaution of closing it tightly. I knew the necessity of being particular about this, because shaving was always a trying ordeal for me, and I could seldom carry it through to a finish without verbal helps. Now this time I was unprotected, but did not suspect it. I had no extraordinary trouble with my razor on this occasion, and was able to worry through with mere mutterings and growlings of an improper sort, but with nothing noisy or emphatic about them—no snapping and barking. Then I put on a shirt. My shirts are an invention of my own. They open in the back, and are buttoned there—when there are buttons. This time the button was missing. My temper jumped up several degrees in a moment, and my remarks rose accordingly, both in loudness and vigor of expression. But I was not troubled, for the bath-room door was a solid one and I supposed it was firmly closed. I flung up the window and threw the shirt out. It fell upon the shrubbery where the people on their way to church could admire it if they wanted to; there was merely fifty feet of grass between the shirt and the passer-by. Still rumbling and thundering distantly, I put on another shirt. Again the button was absent. I augmented my language to meet the emergency, and threw that shirt out of the window. I was too angry—too insane—to examine the third shirt, but put it furiously on. Again the button was absent, and that shirt followed its comrades out of the window. Then I straightened up, gathered my reserves, and let myself go like a cavalry charge. In the midst of that great assault, my eye fell upon that gaping door, and I was paralyzed.

It took me a good while to finish my toilet. I extended the time unnecessarily in trying to make up my mind as to what I would best do in the circumstances. I tried to hope that Mrs. Clemens was asleep, but I knew better. I could not escape by the window. It was narrow, and suited only to shirts. At last I made up my mind to boldly loaf through the bedroom with the air of a person who had not been doing anything. I made half the journey successfully. I did not turn my eyes in her direction, because that would not be safe. It is very difficult to look as if you have not been doing anything when the facts are the other way, and my confidence in my performance oozed steadily out of me as I went along. I was aiming for the left-hand door because it was furthest from my wife. It had never been opened from the day that the house was built, but it seemed a blessed refuge for me now. The bed was this one, wherein I am lying now, and dictating these histories morning after morning with so much serenity. It was this same old elaborately carved black Venetian bedstead— the most comfortable bedstead that ever was, with space enough in it for a family, and carved angels enough surmounting its twisted columns and its headboard and footboard to bring peace to the sleepers, and pleasant dreams. I had to stop in the middle of the room. I hadn't the strength to go on. I believed that I was under accusing eyes—that even the carved angels were inspecting me with an unfriendly gaze. You know how it is when you are convinced that somebody behind you is looking steadily at you. You *have* to turn your face— you can't help it. I turned mine. The bed was placed as it is now, with the foot where the head ought to be. If it had been placed as it should have been, the high headboard would have sheltered me. But the footboard was no sufficient protection, for I could be seen over it. I was exposed. I was wholly without protection. I turned, because I couldn't help it—and my memory of what I saw is still vivid, after all these years.

Against the white pillows I saw the black head—I saw that young and beautiful face; and I saw the gracious eyes with a something in them which I had never seen there before. They were snapping and flashing with indignation. I felt myself crumbling; I felt myself shrinking away to nothing under that accusing gaze. I stood silent under that desolating fire for as much as a minute, I should say—it seemed a very, very long time. Then my wife's lips parted, and from them issued—*my latest bath-room remark*. The language perfect, but

Olivia (Livy) Clemens, 1872 or 1873.

the expression velvety, unpractical, apprenticelike, ignorant, inexperienced, comically inadequate, absurdly weak and unsuited to the great language. In my lifetime I had never heard anything so out of tune, so inharmonious, so incongruous, so ill-suited to each other as were those mighty words set to that feeble music. I tried to keep from laughing, for I was a guilty person in deep need of charity and mercy. I tried to keep from bursting, and I succeeded—until she gravely said, "There, now you know how it sounds."

Then I exploded; the air was filled with my fragments, and you could hear them whiz. I said, "Oh Livy, if it sounds like *that* I will never do it again!"

Then she had to laugh herself. Both of us broke into convulsions, and went on laughing until we were physically exhausted and spiritually reconciled.

##  Be Good, Be Good. *A Poem.*

(1908)

*The recipient of this poem was twelve-year-old Margaret Blackmer, whom Clemens met in Bermuda in 1908. She became a member of his "Aquarium," one of several "angelfish" he visited and corresponded with and considered his surrogate granddaughters.*

Be good, be good, be always good,
And now & then be clever,
But don't you ever be *too* good,
Nor ever be too clever;
For such as be too awful good

They awful lonely are,
And such as often clever be
  Get cut & stung & trodden on by persons of
lesser mental capacity, for this kind do by a law of
their construction regard exhibitions of superior
intellectuality as an offensive impertinence leveled
at their lack of this high gift, & are prompt to resent
such-like exhibitions in the manner above
indicated — & are they justifiable? alas, alas they

(It is not best to go on; I think the line is already longer than it ought to be for real true poetry.)

Mark Twain

## An Innovative Dinner Party Signal System

(from a 1906 autobiographical dictation)

*The Clemens family, expatriates since 1891, rented a "charming mansion" in Paris at 169 rue de l'Université in 1895 and probably in 1894 as well.*

In that pleasant Paris house Mrs. Clemens gathered little dinner companies together once or twice a week, and it goes without saying that in these circumstances my defects had a large chance for display. *Always*, always without fail, as soon as the guests were out of the house, I saw that I had been miscarrying again. Mrs. Clemens explained to me the various things which I had been doing which should have been left undone, and she was always able to say

"I have told you over and over again, yet you do these same things every time, just as if I never had warned you."

The children always waited up to have the joy of overhearing this. Nothing charmed them, nothing delighted them, nothing satisfied their souls like seeing me under discipline. The moment we started up-stairs we would hear scurrying garments, and we knew that those children had been at it again. They had a name for this performance. They called it "dusting-off papa." They were obedient young rascals as a rule, by habit, by training, by long experience; but they drew the line there. They couldn't be persuaded to obey the command to stay out of hearing when I was being dusted off.

At last I had an inspiration. It is astonishing that it had not occurred to me earlier. I said

"Why Livy, you know that dusting me off *after* these dinners is not the wise way. You could dust me off after every dinner for a year and I should always be just as competent to do the forbidden thing at each succeeding dinner as if you had not said a word, because in the meantime I have forgotten all these instructions. I think the correct way is for you to dust me off immediately before the guests arrive, and then I can keep some of it in my head and things will go better."

She recognized that that was wisdom, and that it was a very good idea. Then we set to work to arrange a system of signals to be delivered by her to me during dinner; signals which would indicate definitely which particular crime I was now engaged in, so that I could change to another. Apparently one of the children's most precious joys had come to an end and passed out of their life. I supposed that that was so, but it wasn't. The young unteachables got a screen arranged so that they could be behind it during the dinner and listen for the signals and entertain themselves with them. The system of signals was very simple, but it was very effective. If Mrs. Clemens happened to be so busy, at any time, talking with her elbow-neighbor, that she overlooked something that I was doing, she was sure to get a low-voiced hint from behind that screen in these words:

"Blue card, mamma"; or "red card, mamma"—"green card, mamma"— so that I was under double and triple guard. What the mother didn't notice the children detected for her.

As I say, the signals were quite simple, but very effective. At a hint from behind the screen, Livy would look down the table and say, in a voice full of interest, if not of counterfeited apprehension, "What did you do with the blue card that was on the dressing-table—"

That was enough. I knew what was happening—that I was talking the lady on my right to death and never paying any attention to the one on my left. The blue card meant "Let the lady on your right have a reprieve; destroy the one on your left"; so I would at once go to talking vigorously to the lady on my left. It wouldn't be long till there would be another hint, followed by a remark from Mrs. Clemens which had in it an apparently casual reference to a red card, which meant "Oh, are you going to sit there all the evening and never say anything? Do wake up and talk." So I waked up and drowned the table with talk. We had a number of cards, of different colors, each meaning a definite thing, each calling attention to some crime or other in my common list; and that system was exceedingly useful. It was entirely successful. It was like Buck Fanshaw's riot; it broke up the riot before it got a chance to begin. It headed off crime after crime all through the dinner, and I always came out at the end successful, triumphant, with large praises owing to me, and I got them on the spot.

#  About American Manners

(from a 1906 speech)

What shall we say is the best part, the accepted part, the essential part, of the American gentleman? Let us say it is courtesy and a blemishless character. What is courtesy? Consideration for others. Is there a good deal of it in the American character? So far as I have observed—no. Is it an American characteristic? So far as I have observed, the most striking, the most prominent, the most American of all American characteristics is the poverty of it in the American character. Even the foreigner loses his kindly politeness as soon as we get him Americanized. When we have been abroad among either the naked savages or the clothed civilized, for even so brief a time as a year, the first thing we notice when we get back home is the wanton and unprovoked discourtesies that assail us at every turn. They begin at the customs pier, and they follow us everywhere. Such of you as have been abroad will feel with remembered pangs and cheek-burnings, that I am speaking the truth; the rest of you will confess it some day when you come home from abroad. . . .

I am working hard, day and night, without salary or hope of applause, upon my high and self-appointed task of reforming our national manners, and I ask for your help. Am I polite, do you ask? Well . . . . no, I'm an American myself. Why don't I begin by reforming my own manners? I have already explained that, in the beginning. I said, it is noble to teach one's self; but still nobler to teach others—and less trouble.

# ﷽ Breaking It Gently ﷽

(1870)

"Yes, I remember that anecdote," the Sunday school superintendent said, with the old pathos in his voice and the old sad look in his eyes. "It was about a simple creature named Higgins, that used to haul rock for old Maltby. When the lamented Judge Bagley tripped and fell down the court-house stairs and broke his neck, it was a great question how to break the news to poor Mrs. Bagley. But finally the body was put into Higgins's wagon and he was instructed to take it to Mrs. B., but to be very guarded and discreet in his language, and not break the news to her at once, but do it gradually and gently. When Higgins got there with his sad freight, he shouted till Mrs. Bagley came to the door. Then he said:

"Does the widder Bagley live here?"

"The *widow* Bagley? *No,* Sir!"

"I'll bet she does. But have it your own way. Well, does *Judge* Bagley live here?"

"Yes, Judge Bagley lives here."

"I'll bet he don't. But never mind—it ain't for me to contradict. Is the Judge in?"

"No, not at present."

"I jest expected as much. Because, you know—take hold o' suthin, mum, for I'm a-going to make a little communication, and I reckon maybe it'll jar you some. There's been an accident, mum. I've got the old Judge curled up out here in the wagon—and when you see him you'll acknowledge, yourself, that an inquest is about the only thing that could be a comfort to *him!*"

# Courtesy to Unexpected Visitors

(from a 1906 speech)

At one time in our domestic history we had a colored butler who had a failing. He could never remember to ask people who came to the door to state their business. So I used to suffer a good many calls unnecessarily.

One morning when I was especially busy he brought me a card engraved with a name I did not know. So I said, "What does he wish to see me for?" and Sylvester said, "Ah couldn't ask him, sah; he wuz a genlmun." "Return instantly," I thundered, "and inquire his mission. Ask him what's his game." Well, Sylvester returned with the announcement that he had lightning-rods to sell. "Indeed," said I, "things are coming to a fine pass when lightning-rod agents send up engraved cards." "He has pictures," added Sylvester. "Pictures, indeed! He may be peddling etchings. Has he a Russia leather case?" But Sylvester was too frightened to remember. I said, "I am going down to make it hot for that upstart!"

I went down the stairs, working up my temper all the way. When I got to the parlor I was in a fine frenzy concealed beneath a veneer of frigid courtesy. And when I looked in the door, sure enough he had a Russia leather case in his hand. But I didn't happen to notice that it was our Russia leather case.

And if you'd believe me, that man was sitting with a whole gallery of etchings spread out before him. But I didn't happen to notice that they were our etchings, spread out by some member of my family for some unguessed purpose.

Very curtly I asked the gentleman his business. With a surprised, timid manner he faltered that he had met my wife and daughter at Onteora, and they had asked him to call. Fine lie, I thought, and I froze him.

He seemed to be kind of nonplussed, and sat there fingering the etchings in the case until I told him he needn't bother, because we had those. That pleased him so much that he leaned over, in an embarrassed way, to pick up another from the floor. But I stopped him. I said, "We've got that, too." He seemed pitifully amazed, but I was congratulating myself on my great success.

Finally the gentleman asked where Mr. Winton lived; he'd met him in the mountains, too. So I said I'd show him gladly. And I did on the spot. And when he was gone I felt queer, because there were all his etchings spread out on the floor.

Well, my wife came in and asked me who had been in. I showed her the card, and told her all exultantly. To my dismay she nearly fainted. She told me he had been a most kind friend to them in the country, and had forgotten to tell me that he was expected our way. And she pushed me out of the door, and commanded me to get over to the Wintons in a hurry and get him back.

I came into the drawing-room, where Mrs. Winton was sitting up very stiff in a chair, beating me at my own game. Well, I began to put another light on things. Before many seconds Mrs. Winton saw it was time to change her temperature. In five minutes I had asked the man to luncheon, and she to dinner, and so on.

We made that fellow change his trip and stay a week, and we gave him the time of his life. Why, I don't believe we let him get sober the whole time.

#  At the Funeral

(1881)

Do not criticise the person in whose honor the entertainment is given.

Make no remarks about his equipment. If the handles are plated, it is best to seem to not observe it.

If the odor of the flowers is too oppressive for your comfort, remember that they were not brought there for you, and that the person for whom they were brought suffers no inconvenience from their presence.

Listen, with as intense an expression of attention as you can command, to the official statement of the character and history of the person in whose honor the entertainment is given; and if these statistics should seem to fail to tally with the facts, in places, do not nudge your neighbor, or press your foot upon his toes, or manifest, by any other sign, your awareness that taffy is being distributed.

If the official hopes expressed concerning the person in whose honor the entertainment is given are known by you to be oversized, let it pass—do not interrupt.

At the moving passages, be moved—but only according to the degree of your intimacy with the parties giving the entertainment, or with the party in whose honor the entertainment is given. Where a blood relation sobs, an intimate friend should choke up, a distant acquaintance should sigh, a stranger should merely fumble sympathetically with his handkerchief. Where the occasion is military, the emotions should be graded according to military rank, the highest officer present taking precedence in emotional violence, and the rest modifying their feelings according to their position in the service.

Do not bring your dog.

# ⁘ A Telephonic Conversation ⁙

(1880)

*Clemens had one of the earliest residential telephones installed at his Hartford home about late December 1877. It connected his house with the office of the* Hartford Courant *and allowed him to use the* Courant *as an intermediary in sending and receiving telegrams and conducting other personal business.*

I consider that a conversation by telephone—when you are simply sitting by and not taking any part in that conversation—is one of the solemnest curiosities of this modern life. Yesterday I was writing a deep article on a sublime philosophical subject while such a conversation was going on in the room. I notice that one can always write best when somebody is talking through a telephone close by. Well, the thing began in this way. A member of our household came in and asked me to have our house put into communication with Mr. Bagley's, down town. I have observed, in many cities, that the sex always shrink from calling up the central office themselves. I don't know why, but they do. So I touched the bell, and this talk ensued:—

*Central Office.* [Gruffly.] Hello!

*I.* Is it the Central Office?

*C. O.* Of course it is. What do you want?

*I.* Will you switch me on to the Bagleys, please?

*C. O.* All right. Just keep your ear to the telephone.

Then I heard, *k-look, k-look, k'look—klook-klook-klook-look-look!* then a horrible "gritting" of teeth, and finally a piping female voice: Y-e-s? [Rising inflection.] Did you wish to speak to me?

Without answering, I handed the telephone to the applicant, and sat down.

Then followed that queerest of all the queer things in this world,—a conversation with only one end to it. You hear questions asked; you don't hear the answer. You hear invitations given; you hear no thanks in return. You have listening pauses of dead silence, followed by apparently irrelevant and unjustifiable exclamations of glad surprise, or sorrow, or dismay. You can't make head or tail of the talk, because you never hear anything that the person at the other end of the wire says. Well, I heard the following remarkable series of observations, all from the one tongue, and all shouted,—for you can't ever persuade the sex to speak gently into a telephone:—

Yes? Why, how did *that* happen?

Pause.

What did you say?

Pause.

Oh, no, I don't think it was.

Pause.

*No!* Oh, no, I didn't mean *that.* I meant, put it in while it is still boiling,—or just before it *comes* to a boil.

Pause.

WHAT?

Pause.

I turned it over with a back stitch on the selvage edge.

Pause.

Yes, I like that way, too; but I think it's better to baste it on with Valenciennes or bombazine, or something of that sort. It gives it such an air,—and attracts so much notice.

Pause.

It's forty-ninth Deuteronomy, sixty-fourth to ninety-seventh inclusive. I think we ought all to read it often.

Pause.

Perhaps so; I generally use a hair-pin.

Pause.

What did you say? [*Aside.*] Children, do be quiet!

Pause.

*Oh!* B *flat!* Dear me, I thought you said it was the cat!

Pause.

Since *when?*

Pause.

Why, *I* never heard of it.

Pause.

You astound me! It seems utterly impossible!

Pause.

*Who* did?

Pause.

Good-ness gracious!

Pause.

Well, what *is* this world coming to? Was it right in *church?*

Pause.

And was her *mother* there?

Pause.

Why, Mrs. Bagley, I should have died of humiliation! What did they *do?*

Long pause.

I can't be perfectly sure, because I haven't the notes by me; but I think it goes something like this: te-rolly-loll-loll, loll lolly-loll-loll, O tolly-loll-loll-*lee-ly-li-i*-do! And then *repeat*, you know.

Pause.

Yes, I think it *is* very sweet,—and very solemn and impressive, if you get the andantino and the pianissimo right.

Pause.

Oh, gum-drops, gum-drops! But I never allow them to eat striped candy. And of course they *can't,* till they get their teeth, any way.

Pause.

*What?*

Pause.

Oh, not in the least,—go right on. He's here writing,—it doesn't bother *him.*

Pause.

Very well, I'll come if I can. [*Aside.*] Dear me, how it does tire a person's arm to hold this thing up so long! I wish she'd—

Pause.

Oh, no, not at all; I *like* to talk,—but I'm afraid I'm keeping you from your affairs.

Pause.

Visitors?

Pause.

No, we never use butter on them.

Pause.

Yes, that is a very good way; but all the cook-books say they are very unhealthy when they are out of season. And *he* doesn't like them, any way,—especially canned.

Pause.

Oh, I think that is too high for them; we have never paid over fifty cents a bunch.

Pause.

*Must* you go? Well, *good*-by.

Pause.

Yes, I think so. *Good*-by.

Pause.

Four o'clock, then——I'll be ready. *Good*-by.

Pause.

Thank you ever so much. *Good*-by.

Pause.

Oh, not at all!——just as fresh— *Which?* Oh, I'm glad to hear you say that. *Good*-by.

[Hangs up the telephone and says, "Oh, it *does* tire a person's arm so!"]

A man delivers a single brutal "Good-by," and that is the end of it. Not so with the gentle sex,——I say it in their praise; they cannot abide abruptness.

*Oh, never mind, I reckon I'm good enough just as I am.*

# NOTICE.

## To the next Burglar

There is nothing but plated war[e]
in this house, now and henceforth.
You will find it in that brass thing
in the dining-room over in
the corner by the basket of kitten[s].
If you want the basket, put the
kittens in the brass thing. Do no[t]
make a noise – it disturbs the famil[y].
You will find rubbers in the fro[nt]
hall, by that thing which has the
umbrellas in it, chiffonier, I think the[y]
call it, or pergola, or something like th[at].

Please close the door when you go awa[y]!

Very truly yours

S. L. Clemens

# ❧ Modest Proposals and Judicious Complaints ❧

*Mark Twain's proposals are often good-humored, but some
situations require a firm hand and a liberal application
of irony and invective.*

➜ Nothing so needs reforming as other people's habits.

➜ When I reflect upon the number of dis-agreeable people who I know have gone to a better world, I am moved to lead a different life.

#  A Christmas Wish

(published in the *New York World*, 1890)

To the Editor of The World:

It is my heart-warm and world-embracing Christmas hope and aspiration that all of us—the high, the low, the rich, the poor, the admired, the despised, the loved, the hated, the civilized, the savage—may eventually be gathered together in a heaven of everlasting rest and peace and bliss—except the inventor of the telephone.

Mark Twain.

Hartford, Dec. 23.

Mark Twain created this chart in order to keep track of his household's misbehaving telephone.

#  Proposal Regarding Local Flooding

(published in the *Hartford Courant*, 1873)

To the Editor of the Courant:—

About noon yesterday the Rev. George H. Bigler, one of the oldest and most esteemed citizens of Farmington, left his home in that village to visit his married daughter, Mrs. Eli Sawyer, of Hartford. He came in an open two-horse wagon, and was accompanied by his wife, his youngest son, Thomas, aged 18; his grandchild, Minnie Sawyer, aged 8; and two neighbors, Simon and Ellsworth Oglethorpe, brothers, the former a lawyer and the latter formerly postmaster of Farmington. When the wagon arrived at the junction of Farmington avenue and Forest street, in this city, the guard of warning who should have been on duty there was absent from his post; the party in the wagon glanced up at the semaphore telegraph on the top of Mr. Chamberlin's house, and strangely enough but one of its arms was visible and that was pointing directly north, signifying "No danger." So they turned into Forest street and proceeded on their way. In a little while they found themselves hopelessly entangled among the grading and gas-laying improvements, which have been going on in that street since the inauguration of the Christian Era. They shouted for help and presently made themselves heard; passers-by ran to the vicinity, and as soon as they comprehended the state of the case an alarm was sounded (it is due to Mr. Joseph W. Milligan, grocer, to say that he was the first to get to a fire alarm station and turn the key) and within a few minutes all the bells in the city were clamoring. Thousands and tens of thousands of people gathered to the scene of danger and openly sympathized with the persons in peril. They could do no more, for it would have been foolhardy in the extreme to venture into the street, the mud being at that place from thirty to ninety feet deep on a level, to say nothing of the water.

The wagon made another start, and plowed along desperately until it reached the monument (the first one from Farmington avenue—the one erected to a street commissioner during the middle ages for promising to quit repairing the street—which he basely violated and hence the vindictiveness of the inscription on the shaft). Here, as is known, there is more water than mud; the nearest life-boat station in this part of the street is the one located in front of Mr. George Warner's (new) premises. Captain Hobson and his crew of nine men at once launched a life-boat and started on their errand, notwithstanding it was Sunday and would cause remark; but the wind was blowing a gale by this time, and as it was just the turn of the tide, every thing was against the gallant boys. The boat was swept to leeward of the monument and shivered to atoms against the marble column erected in 1598 to the memory of a Sabbath school procession which disappeared at that spot, dressed with unusual care in the best clothes they had, and were never heard of afterward. Fragments of the life-boat crew washed ashore this morning in the extreme southern end of Forest street, nearly three hundred yards from the scene of the disaster. The party in the wagon were well nigh desperate now. But when hope seemed darkest Capt. Duncan MacAllister of the canal boat George Washington arrived with a ship's compass, a chronometer fifteen minutes slow, and a sack of sea-biscuit and hove them aboard the vehicle, while cheers rent the air from the surging multitude that lined the sidewalks. The Rev. Mr. Bigler and his party seemed greatly encouraged after a brief luncheon. (These crackers were from Johnson and Peterson's bakery and are acknowledged to be the best in this market.) Mr. Bigler now bore away sou-west-by-west-half-west, but his weather harness got fouled, his port check-rein fetched away, and his wagon broached to and went ashore at the base of the monument erected five years ago to commemorate the 1868th annual alteration of the grade. Here the starboard horse began to disappear; Mr. Simon Oglethorpe at once cut away the main rigging, and the animal continued his journey to China. Within five minutes the other horse followed him. There was a heavy sea on by this time, of mud and water mixed, and every third colossal poultice of it that rolled along made a clean breach over the wagon and left the occupants looking like the original Adam before the clay dried.

Hope now departed at once and forever, and it was heartrending to hear the castaways plead for a little drop of limpid water; they were willing to die, they were ready to die, but they wanted to wash first. There was not a dry eye in the vicinity. The awful moment came at last; a great sea of sable mush swept the wagon from stem to stern, then the vehicle plunged once, twice, three times, and disappeared beneath the state with all its precious freight on board.

This is a sad case. I am not writing this letter in order to make a great to-do about the loss of a few unnecessary country people in Forest street, for of course that is too common a thing to excite much attention; but I have an object which makes my letter of moment.

In the first place I wish to discourage the building of monuments in Forest street. Every few years the street commissioner goes out there and deposits sixteen feet of gas pipe (on top of the ground) and straightway the property-holders set up a majestic monument to remember it by. Every year he changes the grade and plagiarizes original chaos, and they monumentalize that. Every now and then somebody gets off soundings there and never comes back to dinner any more, and up goes another monument. The result is that what solid ground there is in that street is all occupied by monuments, now, and it makes no end of trouble. There is only one solid spot left, and I discover that a new length of gas pipe has just been dumped in the street and the ground ravaged in the vicinity, preparatory to burying that piece of tube one of these years. Now, will they not want to commemorate that bit of official energy? You know, yourself, that they will, and away goes the last square yard of firm soil in Forest street. If there had been fewer monuments to get shipwrecked against, the Farmington people and the life-boat crew might all be with us yet.

Secondly, I think there ought to be more lanterns standing on barrels, and more sentinels roosting on the fences along Forest street, to warn strangers.

Thirdly, I think there ought to be at least three more life-boat stations on that street, and a number of miscellaneous rafts, with provisions and literature lashed on them, distributed along here and there.

Fourthly, I think there ought to be a chart of the street made, with the soundings marked on it.

Fifthly, I think the war office ought to establish a signal station in Forest street and put in the Probabilities, "Danger signals are ordered for the lakes, the Gulf of Mexico, the Atlantic seaboard and Forest street, Hartford—the one at Forest street to be nailed up with fifteen inch spikes and remain permanent in all weathers."

Then I shall enjoy living in this soft, retired street even more than I do now, perhaps.

M. T.

Sunday, March 30.

## Complaint about Unreliable Service

(an 1891 letter to the Hartford City Gas Light Company)

Hartford, Feb. 12/91.

Dear Sirs:

Some day you will move me almost to the verge of irritation by your chuckleheaded Goddamned fashion of shutting your Goddamned gas off without giving any notice to your Goddamned parishioners. Several times you have come within an ace of smothering half of this household in their beds & blowing up the other half by this idiotic, not to say criminal, custom of yours. And it has happened again to-day. Haven't you a telephone?

Ys

S L Clemens

##  Notice about a Stolen Umbrella

(published in the *Hartford Courant*, 1875)

TWO HUNDRED AND FIVE DOLLARS REWARD——At the great base ball match on Tuesday, while I was engaged in hurrahing, a small boy walked off with an English-made brown silk UMBRELLA belonging to me, and forgot to bring it back. I will pay $5 for the return of that umbrella in good condition to my house on Farmington avenue. I do not want the boy (in an active state) but will pay two hundred dollars for his remains.

Samuel L. Clemens.

# An Appeal against Injudicious Swearing

(published in the *New York Sun*, 1890)

To the Editor of the Sun—Sir: Doubtless you city people do not mind having your feelings hurt and your self-love blistered, for your horse car and elevated road service train you to patience and humble-mindedness, but with us hayseed folk from the back settlements the case is different. We are so delicate, so sensitive—well, you would never be able to imagine what it is like. An unkind speech shrivels us all up and often makes us cry. Now, the thing which happened to-day a New Yorker would not mind in the least; but I give you my word it almost made me want to go away and be at rest in the cold grave.

I stepped aboard a red Sixth avenue horse car—No. 106—at Sixth avenue and Forty-second street at 11:45 this morning, bound down town. Of course there was no seat—there never is; New Yorkers do not require a seat, but only permission to stand up, and look meek, and be thankful for such little rags of privilege as the good horse-car company may choose to allow them. I stood in the door, behind three ladies. After a moment, the conductor, desiring to pass through and see the passengers, took me by the lapel and said to me with that winning courtesy and politeness which New Yorkers are so accustomed to: "Jesus Christ! what you want to load up the door for? Git back here out of the way!" Those ladies shrank together under the shock, just the same as I did; so I judged they were country people. This conductor was a person about 30 years old, I should say, five feet nine, with blue eyes, a small, dim, unsuccessful moustache, and the general expression of a chicken thief—you may probably have seen him.

I urged him to modify his language, I being from the country and sensitive. He looked upon me with cold and heartless scorn, thus hurting me still more. I said I would report him, and asked him for his number. He said, in a tone which wounded me more than I can tell, "I'll give you a chew of tobacco."

Why, dear sir, if conductors were to talk to us like that out in the country we could never, never bear to ride with them, we are so sensitive. I went up to Sixth avenue and Forty-third street to report him, but there was nobody in the superintendent's office who seemed to want to converse with me. A man with "conductor" on his cap said it wouldn't be any use to try to see the President at that time of day, and intimated, by his manner, not his words, that people with complaints were not popular there, any way.

So I have been obliged to come to you, you see. What I wanted to say to the President of the road was this—and through him say it to the President of the elevated roads—that the conductors ought to be instructed never to swear at country people except when there are no city ones to swear at, and not even then except for practice. Because the country people are sensitive. Conductors need not make any mistake; they can easily tell us from the city people. Could you use your influence to get this small and harmless distinction made in our favor?

Mark Twain.

Saturday, Nov. 8.

# ❧ An Unwanted Magazine Subscription ❧

(1883)

Hartford, Feb. 18/83.

J. W. Bouton, Esq—

D<sup>r</sup> Sir—

Draw & be damned. I subscribed for your Portfolio *one year* & no more. I paid for it. Since then you have thrust it upon me & persecuted me with it at your own risk & in defiance of my several protests.

*You*'ll "draw" on me! The hell you will! Messrs. Slote & Co "refer" you to me. No!—why you can't be in earnest. If *they* refer you to me, of course it must be all right. Dear me, why didn't you get the peanut man on the corner to add HIS authority.

Well, what a marvelous sort of publisher you *must* be, sure enough! You ought to write a book, & call it "How to Combine the Methods of the Highwayman & the Publisher Successfully."

I kiss you, Sweetheart!—Goodbye, good-bye—ta-ta!——ta-ta!

Dearest, I am

Truly Yours

S L Clemens

# On Telephones and Swearing

(from a 1906 autobiographical dictation)

Four or five months ago, in the New York home, I learned by accident that we had been having a good deal of trouble with our telephones. The family get more or less peace and comfort out of concealing vexations from me on account of the infirmities of my temper, and it would be only by accident that I could find out that the telephones were making trouble. Upon inquiry I discovered that my tribe had been following the world's usual custom—they had applied for relief to the Telephone Company's subordinates. This is always a mistake. The only right way is to apply to the President of a corporation; your complaint receives immediate and courteous attention then. I called up the headquarters and asked the President to send some one to my house to listen to a complaint. One of the chief superintendents came—Mr. Scovel. The complaint occupied but a minute of our time. Then he sat by the bed and we smoked and chatted half an hour very pleasantly. I remarked that often and often I would dearly like to use the telephone myself, but didn't dare to do it because when the connection was imperfect I was sure to lose my temper and swear—and while I would like to do that, and would get a good deal of satisfaction out of it, I couldn't venture it because I was aware that by telephone law the Company can remove your telephone if you indulge yourself in that way.

Mr. Scovel gladdened me by informing me that I could allow myself that indulgence without fear of injurious results, for there wouldn't be any, there being a clause in the law which allowed me that valuable privilege. Then he quoted that clause and made me happy.

Two or three months ago I wanted that nameless manuscript heretofore mentioned, and I asked my secretary to call up my New York home on the long-distance and tell my daughter Clara to find that manuscript and send it to me. The line was not in good order, and Miss Lyon found great difficulty in making Clara understand what was wanted. After a deal of shouting back and forth Clara gathered that it was a manuscript that was wanted, and that she would find it among the manuscriptural riffraff in my study somewhere. Then she wanted to know by what sign she would recognize it. She asked for the title of it.

Miss Lyon—using a volume of voice which should have carried to New York without the telephone's help, said—

"It has no title. It begins with a remark."

It took some time to make Clara understand that. Then she said,

"What is the remark?"

Miss Lyon shouted—

"Tell him to go to hell."

*Clara.* "Tell him to go—where?"

*Miss Lyon.* "To hell."

*Clara.* "I can't get it. Spell it."

*Miss Lyon.* "H-E-L-L."

*Clara.* "Oh, *hell.*"

I was troubled, not by the ear-splitting shouting, which I didn't mind, but by the character of the words that were going over that wire and being listened to in every office on it, and for a moment I was scared and said,

"Now they'll take our telephone out, on account of this kind of talk."

But the next moment I was comfortable again, because I remembered that blessed clause in the telephone law which Mr. Scovel had quoted to me, and which said:

"In employing our telephones no subscriber shall be debarred from using his native language."

# About the Proposed Street-Widening

(from an 1874 letter)

Your reference to the sidewalk matter reminds me that I am a citizen of Hartford—a fact which I was forgetting; for since we have perched away up here on top of the hill near heaven I have the feeling of being a sort of scrub angel & am more moved to help shove the clouds around, & get the stars on deck promptly, & keep all things trim & ship-shape in the firmament than to bother myself with the humble insect-interests & occupations of the distant earth. But still, the pecuniary difference between a four-foot & a six-foot side-walk is a thing which even a new angel cannot afford to snub—& if you & Hall carry your point there is one such spirit here on high that will flap his wings & rejoice.

And now I find a squib in my pocket which I wrote before I left Hartford, with a vague idea of laying it before the authorities. I enclose it for fun. . . .

To the City Authorities.

Gentlemen:—Why is it necessary to renew & widen the sidewalk in Farmington avenue from Forest street westward? And why make a six-foot walk all the way to the bridge? I grant you that heretofore there has been need of a wide walk there, because the traffic was very great—but there is no longer such pressing need, for one of the school children who used to go along there is sick, & the other one has moved away.

Resident.

#  Political Economy

(1870)

Political economy is the basis of all good government. The wisest men of all ages have brought to bear upon this subject the——

[Here I was interrupted and informed that a stranger wished to see me down at the door. I went and confronted him, and asked to know his business, struggling all the time to keep a tight rein on my seething political economy ideas, and not let them break away from me or get tangled in their harness. And privately I wished the stranger was in the bottom of the canal with a cargo of wheat on top of him. I was all in a fever, but he was cool. He said he was sorry to disturb me, but as he was passing he noticed that I needed some lightning-rods. I said, "Yes, yes—go on—what about it?" He said there was nothing about it, in particular—nothing except he would like to put them up for me. I am new to housekeeping; have been used to hotels and boarding-houses all my life. Like anybody else of similar experience, I try to appear (to strangers) to be an old housekeeper; consequently I said in an off-hand way that I had been intending for some time to have six or eight lightning-rods put up, but—— The stranger started, and looked inquiringly at me, but I was serene. I thought that if I chanced to make any mistakes he would not catch me by my countenance. He said he would rather have my custom than any man's in town. I said all right, and started off to wrestle with my great subject again, when he called me back and said it would be necessary to know exactly how many "points" I wanted put up, what parts of the house I wanted them on, and what quality of rod I preferred. It was close quarters for a man not used to the exigencies of housekeeping, but I went through creditably, and he probably never suspected that I was a novice. I told

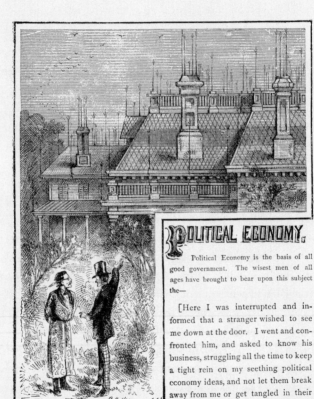

# POLITICAL ECONOMY.

Political Economy is the basis of all good government. The wisest men of all ages have brought to bear upon this subject the—

[Here I was interrupted and informed that a stranger wished to see me down at the door. I went and confronted him, and asked to know his business, struggling all the time to keep a tight rein on my seething political economy ideas, and not let them break away from me or get tangled in their harness. And privately I wished the stranger was in the bottom of the canal with a cargo of wheat on top of him. I was all in a fever, but he was cool. He said he was sorry to disturb me, but

21

From *Mark Twain's Sketches, New and Old* (1875).

him to put up eight "points," and put them all on the roof, and use the best quality of rod. He said he could furnish the "plain" article, at 20 cents a foot; "coppered," 25 cents; "zinc-plated, spiral-twist," at 30 cents, that would stop a streak of lightning any time, no matter where it was bound, and "render its errand harmless and its further progress apocryphal." I said apocryphal was no slouch of a word, emanating from the source it did, but philology aside I liked the spiral-twist and would take that brand. Then he said he *could* make two hundred and fifty feet answer, but to do it right, and make the best job in town of it, and attract the admiration of the just and the unjust alike, and compel all parties to say they never saw a more symmetrical and hypothetical display of lightning-rods since they were born, he supposed he really couldn't get along without four hundred, though he was not vindictive and trusted he was willing to try. I said go ahead and use four hundred and make any kind of a job he pleased out of it, but let me get back to my work. So I got rid of him at last and now, after half an hour spent in getting my train of political economy thoughts coupled together again, I am ready to go on once more.]

richest treasures of their genius, their experience of life, and their learning. The great lights of commercial jurisprudence, international confraternity, and biological deviation, of all ages, all civilizations, and all nationalities, from Zoroaster down to Horace Greeley, have———

[Here I was interrupted again and required to go down and confer further with that lightning-rod man. I hurried off, boiling and surging with prodigious thoughts wombed in words of such majesty that each one of them was in itself a straggling procession of syllables that might be fifteen minutes passing a given point, and once more I confronted him—he so calm and sweet, I so hot and frenzied. He was standing in the contemplative attitude of the Colossus of Rhodes, with one foot on my infant tuberose and the other among my pansies, his hands on his hips, his hat-brim tilted forward, one eye shut and the other gazing critically and admiringly in the direction of my principal chimney. He said now *there* was a state of things to make a man glad to be alive; and added, "I leave it to *you* if you ever saw anything more deliriously picturesque than eight lightning-rods on one chimney?" I said I had no present recollection of anything that transcended it. He said that in his opinion nothing on this earth but Niagara Falls was superior to it in the way of natural scenery. All that was needed now, he verily believed, to make my house a perfect balm to the eye, was to kind of touch up the other chimneys a little and thus "add to the generous *coup d'œil* a soothing uniformity of achievement which would allay the excitement naturally consequent upon the first *coup d'état*." I asked him if he learned to talk out of a book, and if I could borrow it anywhere. He smiled pleasantly, and said that his manner of speaking was not taught in books, and that nothing but familiarity with lightning could enable a man to handle his conversational style with impunity. He then figured up an estimate, and said that about eight more rods scattered about my roof would about fix me right, and he guessed five hundred feet of stuff would do it; and added that the first eight had got a little the start of him, so to speak, and used up a mere trifle of material more than he had calculated on—a hundred feet or along there. I said I was in a dreadful hurry, and I wished we could get this business permanently mapped out so that I could go on with my work. He said: "I *could* have put up those eight rods, and marched off about my business—some men *would* have done it. But no, I said to myself, this man is a stranger to me and I will die before I'll wrong him; there ain't lightning-rods enough on that house, and for one I'll never stir out of my tracks till I've done as I would be done by, and told him so. Stranger, my duty is accomplished; if the recalcitrant and dephlogistic messenger of heaven strikes your——" "There, now, there," I said, "put on the other eight—add five hundred feet of spiral twist—do anything and everything you want to do; but calm your sufferings and try to keep your feelings where you can reach them with the

dictionary. Meanwhile, if we understand each other now, I will go to work again."
I think I have been sitting here a full hour, this time, trying to get back to where
I was when my train of thought was broken up by the last interruption, but I be-
lieve I have accomplished it at last and may venture to proceed again.]

wrestled with this great subject, and the greatest among them have found it a
worthy adversary and one that always comes up fresh and smiling after every
throw. The great Confucius said that he would rather be a profound political
economist than chief of police; Cicero frequently said that political economy
was the grandest consummation that the human mind was capable of con-
suming; and even our own Greeley has said vaguely but forcibly that———

[Here the lightning-rod man sent up another call for me. I went down in a
state of mind bordering on impatience. He said he would rather have died than
interrupt me, but when he was employed to do a job, and that job was expected
to be done in a clean, workmanlike manner, and when it was finished and fatigue urged him to seek the rest and recreation he stood so much in need of,
and he was about to do it, but looked up and saw at a glance that all the cal-
culations had been a little out, and if a thunder storm were to come up and
that house which he felt a personal interest in stood there with nothing on earth
to protect it but sixteen lightning-rods——— "Let us have peace!" I shrieked.
"Put up a hundred and fifty! Put some on the kitchen! Put a dozen on the barn!
Put a couple on the cow!—put one on the cook!—scatter them all over the
persecuted place till it looks like a zinc-plated, spiral-twisted, silver-mounted
cane-brake! Move! Use up all the material you can get your hands on, and when
you run out of lightning-rods put up ram-rods, cam-rods, stair-rods, piston-
rods—*anything* that will pander to your dismal appetite for artificial scenery
and bring respite to my raging brain and healing to my lacerated soul!"
Wholly unmoved—further than to smile sweetly—this iron being simply

turned back his wristbands daintily and said he would now "proceed to hump himself." Well, all that was nearly three hours ago. It is questionable whether I am calm enough yet to write on the noble theme of political economy, but I cannot resist the desire to try, for it is the one subject that is nearest to my heart and dearest to my brain of all this world's philosophy.]

"Political economy is heaven's best boon to man." When the loose but gifted Byron lay in his Venetian exile, he observed that if it could be granted him to go back and live his misspent life over again, he would give his lucid and un-intoxicated intervals to the composition, not of frivolous rhymes, but of es-says upon political economy. Washington loved this exquisite science; such names as Baker, Beckwith, Judson, Smith, are imperishably linked with it; and even imperial Homer, in the ninth book of the Iliad, has said:

> Fiat justitia, ruat cœlum,
> Post mortem unum, ante bellum,
> Hic jacet hoc, ex-parte res,
> Politicum e-conomico est.

The grandeur of these conceptions of the old poet, together with the fe-licity of the wording which clothes them and the sublimity of the imagery whereby they are illustrated, have singled out that stanza and made it more celebrated than any that ever——

["Now, not a word out of you—not a single word. Just state your bill and relapse into impenetrable silence for ever and ever on these premises. Nine hun-dred dollars? Is that all? This check for the amount will be honored at any re-spectable bank in America. What is that multitude of people gathered in the street for? How?—'looking at the lightning-rods!' Bless my life, did they never see any lightning-rods before? Never saw 'such a stack of them on one establishment,' did I understand you to say? I will step down and critically observe this popular ebullition of ignorance."]

THREE DAYS LATER.—We are all about worn out. For four-and-twenty hours our bristling premises were the talk and wonder of the town. The theatres languished, for their happiest scenic inventions were tame and commonplace compared with my lightning-rods. Our street was blocked night and day with spectators, and among them were many who came from the country to see. It was a blessed relief, on the second day, when a thunder storm came up and the lightning began to "go for" my house, as the historian Josephus quaintly phrases it. It cleared the galleries, so to speak. In five minutes there was not a spectator within half a mile of my place; but all the high houses about that distance away were full, windows, roof, and all. And well they might be, for all the falling stars and Fourth of July fireworks of a generation put together and rained down simultaneously out of heaven in one brilliant shower upon one helpless roof, would not have any advantage of the pyrotechnic display that was making my house so magnificently conspicuous in the general gloom of the storm. By actual count the lightning struck at my establishment seven hundred and sixty-four times in forty minutes, but tripped on one of those faithful rods every time and slid down the spiral twist and shot into the earth before it probably had time to be surprised at the way the thing was done. And through all that bombardment only one patch of slates was ripped up, and that was because for a single instant the rods in the vicinity were transporting all the lightning they could possibly accommodate. Well, nothing was ever seen like it since the world began. For one whole day and night not a member of my family stuck his head out of the window but he got the hair snatched off it as smooth as a billiard-ball, and if the reader will believe me not one of us ever dreamt of stirring abroad. But at last the awful siege came to an end—because there was absolutely no more electricity left in the clouds above us within grappling distance of my insatiable rods. *Then* I sallied forth, and gathered daring workmen together, and not a bite or a nap did we take till the premises were utterly stripped of all their terrific armament except just three rods on the house, one on the kitchen, and one on the barn—and behold these remain there even unto this day. And then, and not till then, the people ventured to use our street again. I will remark here, in passing, that during that fearful time I did not continue my essay upon political economy. I am not even yet settled enough in nerve and brain to resume it.

To Whom it May Concern.—Parties having need of three thousand two hundred and eleven feet of best quality zinc-plated spiral-twist lightning-rod stuff, and sixteen hundred and thirty-one silver-tipped points, all in tolerable repair (and, although much worn by use, still equal to any ordinary emergency), can hear of a bargain by addressing the publishers of this magazine.

# Notice. To the Next Burglar

(from a 1908 autobiographical dictation)

*The burglary that elicited this notice occurred at 12:30 A.M. on 18 September 1908 at Clemens's Connecticut estate, Stormfield. Both burglars were captured within a few hours. All of their loot was recovered, some of it immediately, the rest several days later.*

A couple of days after the burglary I put a notice on the front door. By the letters which are arriving now, I find that it has traveled through the European newspapers, and as it had already traveled through the American ones I think that the most of the burglars of this world have read it and will see the wisdom of allowing themselves to be guided by it.

NOTICE.

To the next Burglar.

———

There is nothing but plated ware in this house, now and henceforth. You will find it in that brass thing in the dining room over in the corner by the basket of kittens. If you want the basket, put the kittens in the brass thing. Do not make a noise—it disturbs the family. You will find rubbers in the front hall, by that thing which has the umbrellas in it, chiffonier, I think they call it, or pergola, or something like that.

Please close the door when you go away.

Very truly yours,

S. L. Clemens.

## Suggestion to Persons Entering Heaven

(1910)

*This suggestion is from what is probably Mark Twain's last literary manuscript, written in Bermuda in March 1910, just a few weeks before his death.*

Leave your dog outside. Heaven goes by favor. If it went by merit, you would stay out and the dog would go in.

# Samuel L. Clemens, Litt.D.

## by the LOTOS CLUB New York

Saturday, January 11th, 1908

o nimble and so

full of subtle

Yale, Hon. M.A.
Yale, Hon. Litt.D.
Missouri Univ
Hon. LLD
Missouri Univ
Hon Phi Beta Kappa
Oxford, Hon Litt.D.

## Menu

Innocent Oysters Abroad
Roughing It Soup
Fish, Huckleberry Finn
Joan of Arc Filet of Beef
Jumping Frog, Terrapin
Punch Brothers, Punch
Gilded Age Duck
Hadleyburg Salad
Life on the Mississippi Ice Cream
Prince and the Pauper Cakes
Puddinhead Cheese
White Elephant Coffee

Mark Twain

# ❦⟦ The American Table ⟧❧

Mark Twain shows a decided bias when it comes to
American food and cookery, which is tested by two meals he
suffered through—one at a stagecoach stop en route to Nevada
and another at the home of an indigent cousin.

↬ The true Southern watermelon is a boon apart, and not to be mentioned with commoner things. It is chief of this world's luxuries, king by the grace of God over all the fruits of the earth. When one has tasted it, he knows what the angels eat. It was not a Southern watermelon that Eve took: we know it because she repented.

↬ The widow rung a bell for supper, and you had to come to time. When you got to the table you couldn't go right to eating, but you had to wait for the widow to tuck down her head and grumble a little over the victuals; though there warn't really anything the matter with them. That is, nothing only everything was cooked by itself. In a barrel of odds and ends it is different; things get mixed up, and the juice kind of swaps around, and the things go better.

# Memories of Food on an American Farm

(from an autobiographical sketch, 1897–98)

*The farm was near Florida, Missouri, Clemens's birthplace. It belonged to his uncle and aunt, John and Patsy Quarles. As a boy Clemens spent summers with them, enjoying the company of their eight children as well as their groaning board.*

It was a heavenly place for a boy, that farm of my uncle John's. The house was a double log one, with a spacious floor (roofed in) connecting it with the kitchen. In the summer the table was set in the middle of that shady and breezy floor, and the sumptuous meals—well, it makes me cry to think of them. Fried chicken; roast pig; wild and tame turkeys, ducks, and geese; venison just killed; squirrels, rabbits, pheasants, partridges, prairie chickens; home-made bacon and ham; hot biscuits, hot batter-cakes, hot buckwheat cakes, hot "wheatbread," hot rolls, hot corn pone; fresh corn boiled on the ear, succotash, butter-beans, string beans, tomatoes, peas, Irish potatoes, sweet potatoes; buttermilk, sweet milk, "clabber"; watermelons, musk melons, canteloups—all fresh from the garden—apple pie, peach pie, pumpkin pie, apple dumplings, peach cobbler—I can't remember the rest. The way that the things were cooked was perhaps the main splendor—particularly a certain few of the dishes. For instance, the corn bread, the hot biscuits and wheatbread, and the fried chicken. These things have never been properly cooked in the North—in fact, no one there is able to learn the art, so far as my experience goes. The North thinks it knows how to make corn bread, but this is gross superstition. Perhaps no bread in the world is quite as good as Southern corn bread, and perhaps no bread in the world is quite so bad as the Northern imitation of it. The North seldom tries to fry a chicken, and this is well; the art cannot be learned north of the line of Mason and Dixon, nor anywhere in Europe. This is not hearsay; it is experience that is speaking. In Europe it is imagined that the custom of serving various kinds of bread blazing hot is "American," but that is too broad a spread: it is custom in the South, but is much less than that in the North. In the North and in Europe hot bread is considered unhealthy. This is probably another fussy superstition, like the European superstition that ice-water is unhealthy. Europe does not need ice-water, and does not drink it; and yet, notwithstanding this, its word for it is better than ours, because it describes it, whereas ours doesn't. Europe calls it "iced" water. Our word describes water made from melted ice—a drink which has a characterless taste, and which we have but little acquaintance with.

It seems a pity that the world should throw away so many good things merely because they are unwholesome. I doubt if God has given us any refreshment which, taken in moderation, is unwholesome, except microbes. Yet there are people who strictly deprive themselves of each and every eatable, drinkable and smokable which has in any way acquired a shady reputation. They pay this price for health. And health is all they get for it. They have told me so themselves. How strange it is; it is like paying out your whole fortune for a cow that has gone dry.

## American versus European Food

(from *A Tramp Abroad*, 1880)

*The Clemenses left Hartford in April 1878 to spend sixteen months traveling and shopping in Europe, while allowing Clemens to store up the impressions and experiences he incorporated into* A Tramp Abroad.

The average American's simplest and commonest form of breakfast consists of coffee and beefsteak; well, in Europe, coffee is an unknown beverage. You can get what the European hotel keeper thinks is coffee, but it resembles the real thing as hypocrisy resembles holiness. It is a feeble, characterless, uninspiring sort of stuff, and almost as undrinkable as if it had been made in an American hotel. The milk used for it is what the French call "Christian" milk,—milk which has been baptized.

After a few months' acquaintance with European "coffee," one's mind weakens, and his faith with it, and he begins to wonder if the rich beverage of home, with its clotted layer of yellow cream on top of it is not a mere dream, after all, and a thing which never existed.

Next comes the European bread,—fair enough, good enough, after a fashion, but cold; cold and tough, and unsympathetic; and never any change, never any variety,—always the same tiresome thing.

Next, the butter,—the sham and tasteless butter; no salt in it, and made of goodness knows what.

Then there is the beefsteak. They have it in Europe, but they don't know how to cook it. Neither will they cut it right. It comes on the table in a small, round, pewter platter. It lies in the centre of this platter, in a bordering bed of grease-soaked potatoes; it is the size, shape, and thickness of a man's hand with the thumb and fingers cut off. It is a little overdone, is rather dry, it tastes pretty insipidly, it rouses no enthusiasm.

Imagine a poor exile contemplating that inert thing; and imagine an angel suddenly sweeping down out of a better land and setting before him a mighty porter-house steak an inch and a half thick, hot and sputtering from the griddle; dusted with fragrant pepper; enriched with little melting bits of butter of the most unimpeachable freshness and genuineness; the precious juices of the meat trickling out and joining the gravy, archipelagoed with mushrooms; a township or two of tender, yellowish fat gracing an outlying district of this ample county of beefsteak; the long white bone which divides the sirloin from the tenderloin still in its place; and imagine that the angel also adds a great cup of American home-made coffee, with the cream a-froth on top, some real butter, firm and yellow and fresh, some smoking hot biscuits, a plate of hot buckwheat cakes, with transparent syrup,—could words describe the gratitude of this exile? . . .

It has now been many months, at the present writing, since I have had a nourishing meal, but I shall soon have one,—a modest, private affair, all to myself. I have selected a few dishes, and made out a little bill of fare, which will go home in the steamer that precedes me, and be hot when I arrive—as follows:

Radishes. Baked apples, with cream.
Fried oysters; stewed oysters. Frogs.
American coffee, with real cream.
American butter.
Fried chicken, Southern style.
Porter-house steak.
Saratoga potatoes.
Broiled chicken, American style.

2120

Radishes.
Baked apples, [crossed out] with cream.
Fried oysters; stewed oysters. Frogs.
American coffee, with real cream.

American butter, [crossed out].
Fried chicken, southern style.
Porter-house steak, [crossed out].

Saratoga potatoes.
Broiled chicken, American style.
Hot biscuits, Southern style. [x]
Hot wheat-bread, Southern style. Hot light rolls.
Hot buckwheat cakes.
American [crossed out] toast.
Clear maple syrup.
Virginia bacon, broiled.
[crossed out]
Blue-points, on the half shell.
Cherry-stone clams.
San Francisco mussels, [crossed out] steamed.
Oyster soup. Clam soup.
[Shell] Oysters roasted in the shell—northern style. [x]
Philadelphia terrapin soup.
Soft-shell crabs.
( Connecticut shad.

Baltimore perch.

Brook trout, from Sierra Nevadas.

Lake trout, from Tahoe.

Sheep-head & croakers, from
        New Orleans.
Black bass from the Mississippi.

Mark Twain listed some favorite American foods
in the manuscript of *A Tramp Abroad*.

Hot biscuits, Southern style.

Hot wheat-bread, Southern style.

Hot buckwheat cakes.

American toast. Clear maple syrup.

Virginia bacon, broiled.

Blue points, on the half shell.

Cherry-stone clams.

San Francisco mussels, steamed.

Oyster soup. Clam soup.

Philadelphia Terrapin soup.

Oysters roasted in shell—Northern style.

Soft-shell crabs. Connecticut shad.

Baltimore perch.

Brook trout, from Sierra Nevadas.

Lake trout, from Tahoe.

Sheep-head and croakers, from New Orleans.

Black bass from the Mississippi.

American roast beef.

Roast turkey, Thanksgiving style.

Cranberry sauce. Celery.

Roast wild turkey. Woodcock.

Canvas-back-duck, from Baltimore.

Prairie hens, from Illinois.

Missouri partridges, broiled.

'Possum. Coon.

Boston bacon and beans.

Bacon and greens, Southern style.

Hominy. Boiled onions. Turnips.

Pumpkin. Squash. Asparagus.

Butter beans. Sweet potatoes.

Lettuce. Succotash. String beans.

Mashed potatoes. Catsup.

Boiled potatoes, in their skins.

New potatoes, minus the skins.

Early rose potatoes, roasted in the ashes, Southern style, served hot.

Sliced tomatoes, with sugar or vinegar. Stewed tomatoes.

Green corn, cut from the ear and served with butter and pepper.

Green corn, on the ear.

Hot corn-pone, with chitlings, Southern style.

Hot hoe-cake, Southern style.

Hot egg-bread, Southern style.

Hot light-bread, Southern style.

Buttermilk. Iced sweet milk.

Apple dumplings, with real cream.

Apple pie. Apple fritters.

Apple puffs, Southern style.

Peach cobbler, Southern style.

Peach pie. American mince pie.

Pumpkin pie. Squash pie.

All sorts of American pastry.

Fresh American fruits of all sorts, including strawberries which are not to be doled out as if they were jewelry, but in a more liberal way.

Ice-water—not prepared in the ineffectual goblet, but in the sincere and capable refrigerator.

Americans intending to spend a year or so in European hotels, will do well to copy this bill and carry it along. They will find it an excellent thing to get up an appetite with, in the dispiriting presence of the squalid table d'hôte.

Foreigners cannot enjoy our food, I suppose, any more than we can enjoy theirs. It is not strange; for tastes are made, not born. I might glorify my bill of fare until I was tired; but after all, the Scotchman would shake his head and say, "Where's your haggis?" and the Fijian would sigh and say, "Where's your missionary?"

##  An Inauspicious Meal

(from *Roughing It,* 1872)

Roughing It *was Mark Twain's account of the six years (1861–66) he spent in "variegated vagabondizing" in Nevada, California, and the Sandwich Islands.*

In place of a window there was a square hole about large enough for a man to crawl through, but this had no glass in it. There was no flooring, but the ground was packed hard. There was no stove, but the fire-place served all needful purposes. There were no shelves, no cupboards, no closets. In a corner stood an open sack of flour, and nestling against its base were a couple of black and venerable tin coffee-pots, a tin teapot, a little bag of salt, and a side of bacon.

By the door of the station-keeper's den, outside, was a tin wash-basin, on the ground. Near it was a pail of water and a piece of yellow bar soap, and from the eaves hung a hoary blue woolen shirt, significantly—but this latter was the station-keeper's private towel, and only two persons in all the party might venture to use it—the stage-driver and the conductor. The latter would not, from a sense of decency; the former would not, because he did not choose to encourage the advances of a station-keeper. We had towels—in the valise;

they might as well have been in Sodom and Gomorrah. We (and the conductor) used our handkerchiefs, and the driver his pantaloons and sleeves. By the door, inside, was fastened a small old-fashioned looking-glass frame, with two little fragments of the original mirror lodged down in one corner of it. This arrangement afforded a pleasant double-barreled portrait of you when you looked into it, with one-half of your head set up a couple of inches above the other half. From the glass frame hung the half of a comb by a string—but if I had to describe that patriarch or die, I believe I would order some sample coffins. It had come down from Esau and Samson, and had been accumulating hair ever since—along with certain impurities. In one corner of the room stood three or four rifles and muskets, together with horns and pouches of ammunition. The station-men wore pantaloons of coarse, country-woven stuff, and into the seat and the inside of the legs were sewed ample additions of buckskin, to do duty in place of leggings, when the man rode horseback—so the pants were half dull blue and half yellow, and unspeakably picturesque. The pants were stuffed into the tops of high boots, the heels whereof were armed with great Spanish spurs, whose little iron clogs and chains jingled with every step. The man wore a huge beard and mustachios, an old slouch hat, a blue woolen shirt, no suspenders, no vest, no coat—in a leathern sheath in his belt, a great long "navy" revolver (slung on right side, hammer to the front), and projecting from his boot a horn-handled bowie knife. The furniture of the hut was neither gorgeous nor much in the way. The rocking-chairs and sofas were not present, and never had been, but they were represented by two three-legged stools, a pine-board bench four feet long, and two empty candle-boxes. The table was a greasy board on stilts, and the table-cloth and napkins had not come—and they were not looking for them, either. A battered tin platter, a knife and fork, and a tin pint cup, were at each man's place, and the driver had a queensware saucer that had seen better days. Of course this duke sat at the head of the table. There was one isolated piece of table furniture that bore about it a touching air of grandeur in misfortune. This was the caster. It was German silver, and crippled and rusty, but it was so preposterously out of place there that it was suggestive of a tattered exiled king among barbarians, and the majesty of its native position compelled respect even in its degradation. There was only one cruet left, and that was a stopperless, fly-specked, broken-necked thing, with two inches of vinegar in it, and a dozen preserved flies with their heels up and looking sorry they had invested there.

The station-keeper up-ended a disk of last week's bread, of the shape and size of an old-time cheese, and carved some slabs from it which were as good as Nicolson pavement, and tenderer.

He sliced off a piece of bacon for each man, but only the experienced old hands made out to eat it, for it was condemned army bacon which the United States would not feed to its soldiers in the forts, and the stage company had bought it cheap for the sustenance of their passengers and employés. We may have found this condemned army bacon further out on the plains than the section I am locating it in, but we *found* it—there is no gainsaying that.

Then he poured for us a beverage which he called *"Slumgullion,"* and it is hard to think he was not inspired when he named it. It really pretended to be tea, but there was too much dish-rag, and sand, and old bacon-rind in it to deceive the intelligent traveler. He had no sugar and no milk—not even a spoon to stir the ingredients with.

We could not eat the bread or the meat, nor drink the "slumgullion." And when I looked at that melancholy vinegar-cruet, I thought of the anecdote (a very, very old one, even at that day) of the traveler who sat down to a table which had nothing on it but a mackerel and a pot of mustard. He asked the landlord if this was all. The landlord said:

"*All!* Why, thunder and lightning, I should think there was mackerel enough there for six."

"But I don't like mackerel."

"Oh—then help yourself to the mustard."

In other days I had considered it a good, a very good, anecdote, but there was a dismal plausibility about it, here, that took all the humor out of it.

Our breakfast was before us, but our teeth were idle.

I tasted and smelt, and said I would take coffee, I believed. The station-boss stopped dead still, and glared at me speechless. At last, when he came to, he turned away and said, as one who communes with himself upon a matter too vast to grasp:

"*Coffee!* Well, if that don't go clean ahead of me, I'm d—d!"

We could not eat, and there was no conversation among the hostlers and herdsmen—we all sat at the same board. At least there was no conversation further than a single hurried request, now and then, from one employé to another. It was always in the same form, and always gruffly friendly. Its western freshness and novelty startled me, at first, and interested me; but it presently grew monotonous, and lost its charm. It was:

"Pass the bread, you son of a skunk!" No, I forget—skunk was not the word; it seems to me it was still stronger than that; I know it was, in fact, but it is gone from my memory, apparently. However, it is no matter—probably it was too strong for print, anyway. It is the landmark in my memory which tells me where I first encountered the vigorous new vernacular of the occidental plains and mountains.

We gave up the breakfast, and paid our dollar apiece and went back to our mail-bag bed in the coach, and found comfort in our pipes.

# A Remarkable Dinner

(from *The Gilded Age*, 1873)

*Mark Twain later revealed that this account was based on a meal he himself had eaten at the home of his cousin James J. Lampton, who was the model for Colonel Sellers, the ever-buoyant speculator depicted in* The Gilded Age. *This book was Mark Twain's first novel, written in collaboration with his Hartford neighbor Charles Dudley Warner.*

The Sellers family were just starting to dinner when Washington burst upon them with his surprise. For an instant the Colonel looked nonplussed, and just a bit uncomfortable; and Mrs. Sellers looked actually distressed; but the next moment the head of the house was himself again, and exclaimed:

"All right, my boy, all right—always glad to see you—always glad to hear your voice and take you by the hand. Don't wait for special invitations—that's all nonsense among friends. Just come whenever you can, and come as often as you can—the oftener the better. You can't please us any better than that, Washington; the little woman will tell you so herself. We don't pretend to style. Plain folks, you know—plain folks. Just a plain family dinner, but such as it is, our friends are *always* welcome, I reckon you know that yourself, Washington. Run along, children, run along; Lafayette,* stand off the cat's tail, child,

---

*In those old days the average man called his children after his most revered literary and historical idols; consequently there was hardly a family, at least in the West, but had a Washington in it—and also a Lafayette, a Franklin, and six or eight sounding names from Byron, Scott, and the Bible, if the offspring held out. To visit such a family, was to find one's self confronted by a congress made up of representatives of the imperial myths and the majestic dead of all the ages. There was something thrilling about it, to a stranger, not to say awe inspiring.

"A healthy meal." From the first American edition of *The Gilded Age*, chapter 11.

can't you see what you're doing? — Come, come, come, Roderick Dhu, it isn't nice for little boys to hang onto young gentlemen's coat tails — but never mind him, Washington, he's full of spirits and don't mean any harm. Children will be children, you know. Take the chair next to Mrs. Sellers, Washington — tut, tut, Marie Antoinette, let your brother have the fork if he wants it, you are bigger than he is."

Washington contemplated the banquet, and wondered if he were in his right mind. Was this the plain family dinner? And was it all present? It was soon apparent that this was indeed the dinner: it was all on the table: it consisted of abundance of clear, fresh water, and a basin of raw turnips — nothing more.

Washington stole a glance at Mrs. Sellers's face, and would have given the world, the next moment, if he could have spared her that. The poor woman's face was crimson, and the tears stood in her eyes. Washington did not know what to do. He wished he had never come there and spied out this cruel poverty and brought pain to that poor little lady's heart and shame to her cheek; but he was there, and there was no escape. Col. Sellers hitched back his coat sleeves airily from his wrists as who should say "*Now* for solid enjoyment!" seized a fork, flourished it and began to harpoon turnips and deposit them in the plates before him:

"Let me help you, Washington—Lafayette pass this plate to Washington—ah, well, well, my boy, things are looking pretty bright, now, *I* tell you. Speculation—my! the whole atmosphere's full of money. I wouldn't take three fortunes for one little operation I've got on hand now—have anything from the casters? No? Well, you're right, you're right. Some people like mustard with turnips, but—now there was Baron Poniatowski—Lord, but that man did know how to live!—true Russian you know, Russian to the back bone; I say to my wife, give me a Russian every time, for a table comrade. The Baron used to say, 'Take mustard, Sellers, try the mustard,—a man *can't* know what turnips are in perfection without mustard,' but I always said, 'No, Baron, I'm a plain man, and I want my food plain—none of your embellishments for Eschol Sellers—no made dishes for me![¹] And it's the best way—high living kills more than it cures in this world, you can rest assured of that. Yes indeed, Washington, I've got one little operation on hand that—take some more water—help yourself, won't you?—help yourself, there's plenty of it. You'll find it pretty good, I guess. How does that fruit strike you?"

Washington said he did not know that he had ever tasted better. He did not add that he detested turnips even when they were cooked—loathed them in their natural state. No, he kept this to himself, and praised the turnips to the peril of his soul.

"I thought you'd like them. Examine them—examine them—they'll bear it. See how perfectly firm and juicy they are—they can't start any like them in this part of the country, I can tell you. These are from New Jersey—I imported them myself. They cost like sin, too; but lord bless me, I go in for having the best of a thing, even if it does cost a little more—it's the best economy, in the long run. These are the Early Malcolm—it's a turnip that can't be produced except in just one orchard, and the supply never is up to the demand. Take some more water, Washington—you can't drink too much water with fruit—all the doctors say that. The plague can't come where this article is, my boy!"

"Plague? What plague?"

"What plague, indeed? Why the Asiatic plague that nearly depopulated London a couple of centuries ago."

"But how does that concern us? There is no plague here, I reckon."

"Sh! I've let it out! Well, never mind—just keep it to yourself. Perhaps I oughtn't said anything, but it's *bound* to come out sooner or later, so what is the odds? Old McDowells wouldn't like me to—to—bother it all, I'll just tell the whole thing and let it go. You see, I've been down to St. Louis, and I happened to run across old Dr. McDowells—thinks the world of me, does the doctor. He's a man that keeps himself to himself, and well he may, for he knows that he's got a reputation that covers the whole earth—he won't condescend to open himself out to many people, but lord bless you, he and I are just like brothers; he won't let me go to a hotel when I'm in the city—says I'm the only man that's company to him, and I don't know but there's some truth in it, too, because although I never like to glorify myself and make a great to-do over what I am or what I can do or what I know, I don't mind saying here among friends that I *am* better read up in most sciences, maybe, than the general run of professional men in these days. Well, the other day he let me into a little secret, strictly on the quiet, about this matter of the plague.

"You see it's booming right along in our direction—follows the Gulf Stream, you know, just as all those epidemics do,—and within three months it will be just waltzing through this land like a whirlwind! And whoever it touches can make his will and contract for the funeral. Well you can't *cure* it, you know, but you can prevent it. How? Turnips! that's it! Turnips and water! Nothing like it in the world, old McDowells says, just fill yourself up two or three times a day, and you can snap your fingers at the plague. Sh!—keep mum, but just you confine yourself to that diet and you're all right. I wouldn't have old McDowells know that I told about it for anything—he never would speak to me again. Take some more water, Washington—the more water you drink, the better. Here, let me give you some more of the turnips. No, no, no, now, I insist. There, now. Absorb those. They're mighty sustaining—brim full of nutriment—all the medical books say so. Just eat from four to seven good-sized turnips at a meal, and drink from a pint and a half to a quart of water, and then just sit around a couple of hours and let them ferment. You'll feel like a fighting cock next day."

Fifteen or twenty minutes later the Colonel's tongue was still chattering away—he had piled up several future fortunes out of several incipient "operations" which he had blundered into within the past week, and was now soaring along through some brilliant expectations born of late promising experiments upon the lacking ingredient of the eye-water. And at such a time Washington ought to have been a rapt and enthusiastic listener, but he was not, for two matters disturbed his mind and distracted his attention. One was, that he discovered, to his confusion and shame, that in allowing himself to be helped a second time to the turnips, he had robbed those hungry children. He had not needed the dreadful "fruit," and had not wanted it; and when he saw the pathetic sorrow in their faces when they asked for more and there was no more to give them, he hated himself for his stupidity and pitied the famishing young things with all his heart. The other matter that disturbed him was the dire inflation that had begun in his stomach. It grew and grew, it became more and more insupportable. Evidently the turnips were "fermenting." He forced himself to sit still as long as he could, but his anguish conquered him at last.

John T. Raymond's portrayal of the irrepressible Colonel Sellers
first made Mark Twain's *Gilded Age* play a popular success in 1874.
Raymond toured in the role and staged revivals for twelve years. He is shown
here with the turnips that figured in one of the play's best-known scenes.
(Courtesy of Kevin Mac Donnell.)

He rose in the midst of the Colonel's talk and excused himself on the plea of a previous engagement. The Colonel followed him to the door, promising over and over again that he would use his influence to get some of the Early Malcolms for him, and insisting that he should not be such a stranger but come and take pot-luck with him every chance he got. Washington was glad enough to get away and feel free again. He immediately bent his steps toward home.

In bed he passed an hour that threatened to turn his hair gray, and then a blessed calm settled down upon him that filled his heart with gratitude. Weak and languid, he made shift to turn himself about and seek rest and sleep; and as his soul hovered upon the brink of unconsciousness, he heaved a long, deep sigh, and said to himself that in his heart he had cursed the Colonel's preventive of rheumatism, before, and now *let* the plague come if it must—he was done with preventives; if ever any man beguiled him with turnips and water again, let him die the death.

## Food and Scenery

(from *Roughing It*, 1872)

The accustomed coach life began again, now, and by midnight it almost seemed as if we never had been out of our snuggery among the mail-sacks at all. We had made one alteration, however. We had provided enough bread, boiled ham and hard boiled eggs to last double the six hundred miles of staging we had still to do.

And it was comfort in those succeeding days to sit up and contemplate the majestic panorama of mountains and valleys spread out below us and eat ham and hard boiled eggs while our spiritual natures reveled alternately in rainbows, thunderstorms, and peerless sunsets. Nothing helps scenery like ham and eggs. Ham and eggs, and after these a pipe—an old, rank, delicious pipe—ham and eggs and scenery, a "down grade," a flying coach, a fragrant pipe and a contented heart—these make happiness. It is what all the ages have struggled for.

# 4 ❦[ Travel Manners ]❧

Mark Twain was a great peripatetic. Starting at the age of
seventeen, he traveled America from coast to coast and then went farther
afield: he visited five continents, crossed the Atlantic twenty-nine times,
and made one complete round-the-world circuit on a lecture tour. In his
travel books he presented acutely observed vignettes of travel behavior
that helped to define the image of the American abroad.

→ Travel is fatal to prejudice, bigotry and narrow-mindedness, and many of our people need it sorely on these accounts. Broad, wholesome, charitable views of men and things can not be acquired by vegetating in one little corner of the earth all one's lifetime.

→ The gentle reader will never, never know what a consummate ass he can become, until he goes abroad.

#  Traveling in Close Quarters

(from *Roughing It*, 1872)

Our coach was a great swinging and swaying stage, of the most sumptuous description—an imposing cradle on wheels. It was drawn by six handsome horses, and by the side of the driver sat the "conductor," the legitimate captain of the craft; for it was his business to take charge and care of the mails, baggage, express matter, and passengers. We three were the only passengers, this trip. We sat on the back seat, inside. About all the rest of the coach was full of mail-bags—for we had three days' delayed mails with us. Almost touching our knees, a perpendicular wall of mail matter rose up to the roof. There was a great pile of it strapped on top of the stage, and both the fore and hind boots were full. We had twenty-seven hundred pounds of it aboard, the driver said—"a little for Brigham, and Carson, and 'Frisco, but the heft of it for the Injuns, which is powerful troublesome 'thout they get plenty of truck to read." But as he just then got up a fearful convulsion of his countenance which was suggestive of a wink being swallowed by an earthquake, we guessed that his remark was intended to be facetious, and to mean that we would unload the most of our mail matter somewhere on the Plains and leave it to the Indians, or whosoever wanted it.

We changed horses every ten miles, all day long, and fairly flew over the hard, level road. We jumped out and stretched our legs every time the coach stopped, and so the night found us still vivacious and unfatigued.

After supper a woman got in, who lived about fifty miles further on, and we three had to take turns at sitting outside with the driver and conductor. Apparently she was not a talkative woman. She would sit there in the gathering twilight and fasten her steadfast eyes on a mosquito rooting into her arm, and slowly she would raise her other hand till she had got his range, and then she would launch a slap at him that would have jolted a cow; and after that she would sit and contemplate the corpse with tranquil satisfaction—for she never missed her mosquito; she was a dead shot at short range. She never removed a carcase, but left them there for bait. I sat by this grim Sphynx and watched her kill thirty or forty mosquitoes—watched her, and waited for her to say something, but she never did. So I finally opened the conversation myself. I said:

"The mosquitoes are pretty bad, about here, madam."

"You bet!"

"What did I understand you to say, madam?"

"You BET!"

Then she cheered up, and faced around and said:

"Danged if I didn't begin to think you fellers was deef and dumb. I did, b' gosh. Here I've sot, and sot, and sot, a bust'n muskeeters and wonderin' what was ailin' ye. Fust I thot you was deef and dumb, then I thot you was sick or crazy, or suthin', and then by and by I begin to reckon you was a passel of sickly fools that couldn't think of nothing to say. Wher'd ye come from?"

The Sphynx was a Sphynx no more! The fountains of her great deep were broken up, and she rained the nine parts of speech forty days and forty nights, metaphorically speaking, and buried us under a desolating deluge of trivial gossip that left not a crag or pinnacle of rejoinder projecting above the tossing waste of dislocated grammar and decomposed pronunciation!

How we suffered, suffered, suffered! She went on, hour after hour, till I was sorry I ever opened the mosquito question and gave her a start. She never did stop again until she got to her journey's end toward daylight; and then she stirred us up as she was leaving the stage (for we were nodding, by that time), and said:

"Now you git out at Cottonwood, you fellers, and lay over a couple o' days, and I'll be along some time to-night, and if I can do ye any good by edgin' in a word now and then, I'm right thar. Folks 'll tell you 't I've always ben kind o' offish and partic'lar for a gal that's raised in the woods, and I *am,* with the rag-tag and bob-tail, and a gal *has* to be, if she wants to *be* anything, but when people comes along which is my equals, I reckon I'm a pretty sociable heifer after all."

We resolved not to "lay by at Cottonwood."

## 🙦 Communicating with the Locals 🙧

(from *The Innocents Abroad,* 1869)

We have had a bath in Milan, in a public bath-house. They were going to put all three of us in one bath-tub, but we objected. Each of us had an Italian farm on his back. We could have felt affluent if we had been officially surveyed and fenced in. We chose to have three bath-tubs, and large ones—tubs suited to the dignity of aristocrats who had real estate, and brought it with them. After we were stripped and had taken the first chilly dash, we discovered that haunting atrocity that has embittered our lives in so many cities and villages of Italy and France—there was no soap. I called. A woman answered, and I barely had time to throw myself against the door—she would have been in, in another second. I said:

"Beware, woman! Go away from here—go away, now, or it will be the worse for you. I am an unprotected male, but I will preserve my honor at the peril of my life!"

These words must have frightened her, for she skurried away very fast. Dan's voice rose on the air:

"Oh, bring some soap, why don't you!"

The reply was Italian. Dan resumed:

"Soap, you know—soap. That is what I want—soap. S-o-a-p, soap; s-o-p-e, soap; s-o-u-p, soap. Hurry up! I don't know how you Irish spell it, but I want it. Spell it to suit yourself, but fetch it. I'm freezing."

I heard the doctor say, impressively:

"Dan, how often have we told you that these foreigners cannot understand English? Why will you not depend upon us? Why will you not tell *us* what you want, and let us ask for it in the language of the country? It would save us a great deal of the humiliation your reprehensible ignorance causes us. I will address this person in his mother tongue: 'Here, cospetto! corpo di Bacco! Sacramento! Solferino!—Soap, you son of a gun!' Dan, if you would let *us* talk for you, you would never expose your ignorant vulgarity."

Even this fluent discharge of Italian did not bring the soap at once, but there was a good reason for it. There was not such an article about the establishment. It is my belief that there never had been. They had to send far up town, and to several different places before they finally got it, so they said. We had to wait twenty or thirty minutes. The same thing had occurred the evening before, at the hotel. I think I have divined the reason for this state of things at last. The English know how to travel comfortably, and they carry soap with them; other foreigners do not use the article.

At every hotel we stop at we always have to send out for soap, at the last moment, when we are grooming ourselves for dinner, and they put it in the bill along with the candles and other nonsense. In Marseilles they make half the fancy toilet soap we consume in America, but the Marseillaise only have a vague theoretical idea of its use, which they have obtained from books of travel, just as they have acquired an uncertain notion of clean shirts, and the peculiarities of the gorilla, and other curious matters. This reminds me of poor Blucher's note to the landlord in Paris:

"Paris, le 7 Juillet.

"*Monsieur le Landlord*—Sir: *Pourquoi* don't you *mettez* some *savon* in your bed-chambers? *Est-ce que vous pensez* I will steal it? *La nuit passée* you charged me *pour deux chandelles* when I only had one; *hier vous avez* charged me *avec glace* when I had none at all; *tout les jours* you are coming some fresh game or other on me, *mais vous ne pouvez pas* play this *savon* dodge on me twice. *Savon* is a necessary *de la vie* to any body but a Frenchman, *et je l'aurai hors de cet hôtel* or make trouble. You hear *me. Allons.*

Blucher."

I remonstrated against the sending of this note, because it was so mixed up that the landlord would never be able to make head or tail of it; but Blucher said he guessed the old man could read the French of it and average the rest.

## A Night Excursion in a Hotel Room

(from *A Tramp Abroad*, 1880)

When we got back to the hotel I wound and set the pedometer and put it in my pocket, for I was to carry it next day and keep record of the miles we made. The work which we had given the instrument to do during the day which had just closed, had not fatigued it perceptibly.

We were in bed by ten, for we wanted to be up and away on our tramp homeward with the dawn. I hung fire, but Harris went to sleep at once. I hate a man who goes to sleep at once; there is a sort of indefinable something about it which is not exactly an insult, and yet is an insolence; and one which is hard to bear, too. I lay there fretting over this injury, and trying to go to sleep; but the harder

TRAVEL MANNERS — 87

"Return in war-paint." The author in full—if unorthodox—
travel regalia. From the first American edition of
*The Innocents Abroad*, chapter 13.

I tried, the wider awake I grew. I got to feeling very lonely in the dark, with
no company but an undigested dinner. My mind got a start by and by, and began to consider the beginning of every subject which has ever been thought
of; but it never went further than the beginning; it was touch and go; it fled
from topic to topic with a frantic speed. At the end of an hour my head was in
a perfect whirl and I was dead tired, fagged out.

The fatigue was so great that it presently began to make some head against
the nervous excitement; while imagining myself wide awake, I would really
doze into momentary unconsciousnesses, and come suddenly out of them with
a physical jerk which nearly wrenched my joints apart,—the delusion of the

instant being that I was tumbling backwards over a precipice. After I had fallen over eight or nine precipices and thus found out that one half of my brain had been asleep eight or nine times without the wide-awake, hard-working other half suspecting it, the periodical unconsciousnesses began to extend their spell gradually over more of my brain-territory, and at last I sank into a drowse which grew deeper and deeper and was doubtless just on the very point of becoming a solid, blessed, dreamless stupor, when,—what was that?

My dulled faculties dragged themselves partly back to life and took a receptive attitude. Now out of an immense, a limitless distance, came a something which grew and grew, and approached, and presently was recognizable as a sound,—it had rather seemed to be a feeling, before. This sound was a mile away, now—perhaps it was the murmur of a storm; and now it was nearer,—not a quarter of a mile away; was it the muffled rasping and grinding of distant machinery? No, it came still nearer; was it the measured tramp of a marching troop? But it came nearer still, and still nearer,—and at last it was right in the room: it was merely a mouse gnawing the wood-work. So I had held my breath all that time for such a trifle.

Well, what was done could not be helped; I would go to sleep at once and make up the lost time. That was a thoughtless thought. Without intending it,—hardly knowing it,—I fell to listening intently to that sound, and even unconsciously counting the strokes of the mouse's nutmeg-grater. Presently I was deriving exquisite suffering from this employment, yet maybe I could have endured it if the mouse had attended steadily to his work; but he did not do that; he stopped every now and then, and I suffered more while waiting and listening for him to begin again than I did while he was gnawing. Along at first I was mentally offering a reward of five,—six,—seven,—ten—dollars for that mouse; but toward the last I was offering rewards which were entirely beyond my means. I close-reefed my ears,—that is to say, I bent the flaps of them down and furled them into five or six folds, and pressed them against the hearing-orifice,—but it did no good: the faculty was so sharpened by nervous excitement that it was become a microphone and could hear through the overlays without trouble.

My anger grew to a frenzy. I finally did what all persons before me have done, clear back to Adam,—resolved to throw something. I reached down and got my walking shoes, then sat up in bed and listened, in order to exactly locate the noise. But I couldn't do it; it was as unlocatable as a cricket's noise; and where one thinks that that is, is always the very place where it isn't. So I presently hurled a shoe at random, and with a vicious vigor. It struck the wall over Harris's head and fell down on him; I had not imagined I could throw so far. It woke Harris, and I was glad of it until I found he was not angry; then I was sorry. He soon went to sleep again, which pleased me; but straightway the mouse began again, which roused my temper once more. I did not want to wake Harris a second time, but the gnawing continued until I was compelled to throw the other shoe. This time I broke a mirror,—there were two in the room,— I got the largest one, of course. Harris woke again, but did not complain, and I was sorrier than ever. I resolved that I would suffer all possible torture before I would disturb him a third time.

The mouse eventually retired, and by and by I was sinking to sleep, when a clock began to strike; I counted, till it was done, and was about to drowse again when another clock began; I counted; then the two great Rathhaus clock angels began to send forth soft, rich, melodious blasts from their long trumpets. I had never heard anything that was so lovely, or weird, or mysterious,— but when they got to blowing the quarter-hours, they seemed to me to be overdoing the thing. Every time I dropped off for a moment, a new noise woke me. Each time I woke I missed my coverlet, and had to reach down to the floor and get it again.

At last all sleepiness forsook me. I recognized the fact that I was hopelessly and permanently wide awake. Wide awake, and feverish and thirsty. When I had lain tossing there as long as I could endure it, it occurred to me that it would be a good idea to dress and go out in the great square and take a refreshing wash in the fountain, and smoke and reflect there until the remnant of the night was gone.

I believed I could dress in the dark without waking Harris. I had banished my shoes after the mouse, but my slippers would do for a summer night. So I rose softly, and gradually got on everything,—down to one sock. I couldn't seem to get on the track of that sock, any way I could fix it. But I had to have it; so I went down on my hands and knees, with one slipper on and the other in my hand, and began to paw gently around and rake the floor, but with no success. I enlarged my circle, and went on pawing and raking. With every pressure of my knee, how the floor creaked! and every time I chanced to rake against any article, it seemed to give out thirty-five or thirty-six times more noise than it would have done in the day time. In those cases I always stopped and held my breath till I was sure Harris had not awakened,—then I crept along again. I moved on and on, but I could not find the sock; I could not seem to find anything but furniture. I could not remember that there was much furniture in the room when I went to bed, but the place was alive with it now,—especially chairs,—chairs everywhere,—had a couple of families moved in, in the mean time? And I never could seem to *glance* on one of those chairs, but always struck it full and square with my head. My temper rose, by steady and sure degrees, and as I pawed on and on, I fell to making vicious comments under my breath.

Finally, with a venomous access of irritation, I said I would leave without the sock; so I rose up and made straight for the door,—as I supposed,—and suddenly confronted my dim spectral image in the unbroken mirror. It startled the breath out of me, for an instant; it also showed me that I was lost, and had no sort of idea where I was. When I realized this, I was so angry that I had to sit down on the floor and take hold of something to keep from lifting the roof off with an explosion of opinion. If there had been only one mirror, it might possibly have helped to locate me; but there were two, and two were as bad as a thousand; besides these were on opposite sides of the room. I could see the dim blur of the windows, but in my turned-around condition they were exactly where they ought not to be, and so they only confused me instead of helping me.

I started to get up, and knocked down an umbrella; it made a noise like a pistol-shot when it struck that hard, slick carpetless floor; I grated my teeth and held my breath,—Harris did not stir. I set the umbrella slowly and carefully on end against the wall, but as soon as I took my hand away, its heel slipped from under it, and down it came again with another bang. I shrunk together and listened a moment in silent fury,—no harm done, everything quiet. With the most painstaking care and nicety I stood the umbrella up once more, took my hand away, and down it came again.

I have been strictly reared, but if it had not been so dark and solemn and awful there in that lonely vast room, I do believe I should have said something then which could not be put into a Sunday School book without injuring the sale of it. If my reasoning powers had not been already sapped dry by my harassments, I would have known better than to try to set an umbrella on end on one of those glassy German floors in the dark; it can't be done in the daytime without four failures to one success. I had one comfort, though,—Harris was yet still and silent,—he had not stirred.

The umbrella could not locate me,—there were four standing around the room, and all alike. I thought I would feel along the wall and find the door in that way. I rose up and began this operation, but raked down a picture. It was not a large one, but it made noise enough for a panorama. Harris gave out no sound, but I felt that if I experimented any further with the pictures I should be sure to wake him. Better give up trying to get out. Yes, I would find King Arthur's Round Table once more,—I had already found it several times,— and use it for a base of departure on an exploring tour for my bed; if I could find my bed I could then find my water pitcher; I would quench my raging thirst and turn in. So I started on my hands and knees, because I could go faster that way, and with more confidence, too, and not knock down things. By and by I found the table,—with my head,—rubbed the bruise a little, then rose up and started, with hands abroad and fingers spread, to balance myself. I found a chair; then the wall; then another chair; then a sofa; then an alpenstock, then another sofa; this confounded me, for I had thought there was only one sofa. I hunted up the table again and took a fresh start; found some more chairs.

It occurred to me, now, as it ought to have done before, that as the table was round, it was therefore of no value as a base to aim from; so I moved off once more, and at random among the wilderness of chairs and sofas,—wandered off into unfamiliar regions, and presently knocked a candlestick off a mantel-piece; grabbed at the candlestick and knocked off a lamp; grabbed at the lamp and knocked off a water-pitcher with a rattling crash, and thought to myself, "I've found you at last,—I judged I was close upon you." Harris shouted "murder," and "thieves," and finished with "I'm absolutely drowned."

The crash had roused the house. Mr. X. pranced in, in his long night garment, with a candle, young Z. after him with another candle; a procession swept in at another door, with candles and lanterns,—landlord and two German guests in their nightgowns, and a chambermaid in hers.

I looked around; I was at Harris's bed, a Sabbath day's journey from my own. There was only one sofa; it was against the wall; there was only one chair where a body could get at it,—I had been revolving around it like a planet, and colliding with it like a comet half the night.

I explained how I had been employing myself, and why. Then the landlord's party left, and the rest of us set about our preparations for breakfast, for the dawn was ready to break. I glanced furtively at my pedometer, and found I had made 47 miles. But I did not care, for I had come out for a pedestrian tour anyway.

The MILK DIET **UNFAILING WEIGHT BUILDER**
**HOW IT WILL CURE YOU**

# PHYSICAL CULTURE

MAY
20 Cents

## MARK TWAIN
*Pioneer in Diet and Health*

## BERNARD SHAW
on *"Shall We Whip Children"*

# ❦❲ Health and Diet ❳❧

---

*Over the years, Mark Twain experimented with a variety of
health and diet regimes but always came back to his own admittedly
eccentric practices. When it came to the health of their children,
however, the Clemenses were concerned and doting parents,
quick to call in the family doctor.*

→ He had had much experience of physicians, and said "the only way to keep your health is to eat what you don't want, drink what you don't like, and do what you'd druther not."

→ As an example to others, and not that I care for moderation myself, it has always been my rule never to smoke when asleep, and never to refrain when awake.

# Young Sam Clemens and Old-Time Doctoring

(from an autobiographical sketch, 1897–98)

Beyond the road where the snakes sunned themselves was a dense young thicket, and through it a dim-lighted path led a quarter of a mile; then out of the dimness one emerged abruptly upon a level great prairie which was covered with wild strawberry-plants, vividly starred with prairie pinks, and walled in on all sides by forests. The strawberries were fragrant and fine, and in the season we were generally there in the crisp freshness of the early morning, while the dew-beads still sparkled upon the grass and the woods were ringing with the first songs of the birds.

Down the forest slopes to the left were the swings. They were made of bark stripped from hickory saplings. When they became dry they were dangerous. They usually broke when a child was forty feet in the air, and this was why so many bones had to be mended every year. I had no ill-luck myself, but none of my cousins escaped. There were eight of them, and at one time and another they broke fourteen arms among them. But it cost next to nothing, for the doctor worked by the year—$25 for the whole family. I remember two of the Florida doctors, Chowning and Meredith. They not only tended an entire family for $25 a year, but furnished the medicines themselves. Good measure, too. Only the largest persons could hold a whole dose. Castor-oil was the principal beverage. The dose was half a dipperful, with half a dipperful of New Orleans molasses added to help it down and make it taste good, which it never did. The next standby was calomel; the next, rhubarb; and the next, jalap. Then they bled the patient, and put mustard-plasters on him. It was a dreadful system, and yet the death-rate was not heavy. The calomel was nearly sure to salivate the patient and cost him some of his teeth. There were no dentists. When teeth became touched with decay or were otherwise ailing, the doctor knew of but one thing to do: he fetched his tongs and dragged them out. If the jaw remained, it was not his fault.

Doctors were not called, in cases of ordinary illness; the family's grandmother attended to those. Every old woman was a doctor, and gathered her own medicines in the woods, and knew how to compound doses that would stir the vitals of a cast-iron dog. And then there was the "Indian doctor"; a grave savage, remnant of his tribe, deeply read in the mysteries of nature and the secret properties of herbs; and most backwoodsmen had high faith in his powers and could tell of wonderful cures achieved by him. In Mauritius, away off yonder in the solitudes of the Indian Ocean, there is a person who answers to our Indian doctor of the old times. He is a negro, and has had no teaching as a doctor, yet there is one disease which he is master of and can cure, and the doctors can't. They send for him when they have a case. It is a child's disease of a strange and deadly sort, and the negro cures it with a herb medicine which he makes, himself, from a prescription which has come down to him from his father and grandfather. He will not let any one see it. He keeps the secret of its components to himself, and it is feared that he will die without divulging it; then there will be consternation in Mauritius. I was told these things by the people there, in 1896.

We had the "faith doctor," too, in those early days—a woman. Her specialty was toothache. She was a farmer's old wife, and lived five miles from Hannibal. She would lay her hand on the patient's jaw and say "Believe!" and the cure was prompt. Mrs. Utterback. I remember her very well. Twice I rode out there behind my mother, horseback, and saw the cure performed. My mother was the patient.

Dr. Meredith removed to Hannibal, by and by, and was our family physician there, and saved my life several times. Still, he was a good man and meant well. Let it go.

I was always told that I was a sickly and precarious and tiresome and uncertain child, and lived mainly on allopathic medicines during the first seven years of my life. I asked my mother about this, in her old age—she was in her 88th year—and said:

"I suppose that during all that time you were uneasy about me?"

"Yes, the whole time."

"Afraid I wouldn't live?"

After a reflective pause—ostensibly to think out the facts—

"No—afraid you would."

## The "Wake-Up-Jake"

(1863)

A few days ago I fell a victim to my natural curiosity and my solicitude for the public weal. Everybody had something to say about "wake-up-Jake." If a man was low-spirited; if his appetite failed him; if he did not sleep well at night; if he were costive; if he were bilious; or in love; or in any other kind of trouble; or if he doubted the fidelity of his friends or the efficacy of his religion, there was always some one at his elbow to whisper, "Take a 'wake-up,' my boy." I sought to fathom the mystery, but all I could make out of it was that the "Wake-up Jake" was a medicine as powerful as "the servants of the lamp," the secret of whose decoction was hidden away in Dr. Ellis' breast. I was not aware that I had any use for the wonderful "wake-up," but then I felt it to be my duty to try it, in order that a suffering public might profit by my experience—and I would cheerfully see that public suffer perdition before I would try it again. I called upon Dr. Ellis with the air of a man who would create the impression that he is not so much of an ass as he looks, and demanded a "Wake-up-Jake" as unostentatiously as if that species of refreshment were not at all new to me. The Doctor hesitated a moment, and then fixed up as repulsive a mixture as ever was stirred together in a table-spoon. I swallowed the nauseous mess, and that one meal sufficed me for the space of forty-eight hours. And during all that time, I could not have enjoyed a viler taste in my mouth if I had swallowed a slaughter-house. I lay down with all my clothes on, and with an utter indifference to my fate here or hereafter, and slept like a statue from six o'clock until noon. I got up, then, the sickest man that ever yearned to vomit and couldn't. All the dead and decaying matter in nature seemed buried in my stomach, and I "heaved, and retched, and heaved again," but I could not compass a resurrection—my dead would not come forth. Finally, after rumbling, and growling, and producing agony and chaos within me for many hours, the dreadful dose began its work, and for the space of twelve hours it vomited me, and purged me, and likewise caused me to bleed at the nose.

I came out of that siege as weak as an infant, and went to the bath with Palmer, of Wells, Fargo & Co., and it was well I had company, for it was about all he could do to keep me from boiling the remnant of my life out in the hot steam. I had reached that stage wherein a man experiences a solemn indifference as to whether school keeps or not. Since then, I have gradually regained my strength and my appetite, and am now animated by a higher degree of vigor than I have felt for many a day. 'Tis well. This result seduces many a man into taking a second, and even a third "wake-up-Jake," but I think I can worry along without any more of them. I am about as thoroughly waked up now as I care to be. My stomach never had such a scouring out since I was born. I feel like a jug. If I could get young Wilson or the Unreliable to take a "wake-up-Jake," I would do it, of course, but I shall never swallow another myself—I would sooner have a locomotive travel through me. And besides,

I never intend to experiment in physic any more, just out of idle curiosity. A "wake-up-Jake" will furbish a man's machinery up and give him a fresh start in the world—but I feel I shall never need anything of that sort any more. It would put robust health, and life and vim into young Wilson and the Unreliable—but then they always look with suspicion upon any suggestion that I make.

##  A Healthful Cocktail

(an 1874 letter to Olivia Clemens)

Nothing but *Angostura* bitters will do.

(SLC/MT)          FARMINGTON AVENUE, HARTFORD.

London, Jan 2.

Livy my darling, I want you to be sure & remember to have, in the bath-room, when I arrive, a bottle of Scotch whisky, a lemon, some crushed sugar, & a bottle of *Angostura bitters*. Ever since I have been in London I have taken in a wineglass what is called a cock-tail (made with those ingredients,) before breakfast, before dinner, & just before going to bed. It was recommended by the surgeon of the "City of Chester" & was a most happy thought. To it I attribute the fact that up to this day my digestion has been wonderful—simply *perfect*. It remains day after day & week after week as regular as a clock. Now my dear, if you will give the order *now*, to have those things put in the bath-room & *left* there till I come, they will *be* there when I arrive. Will you? I love to write about arriving—it seems as if it were to be tomorrow. And I love to picture myself ringing the bell, at midnight—then a pause of a second or two—then the turning of the bolt, & "Who is it?"—then ever so many kisses—then you & I in the bath-room, I drinking my cock-tail & undressing, & you standing by—then to bed, and—everything happy & jolly as it should be. I *do* love & honor you, my darling.

Saml.

Detail of original drawing by Bernard Partridge, depicting Mr. Punch (of the English humor magazine *Punch*) toasting Mark Twain. Presented to the author at a dinner in his honor on 9 July 1907.

# ❦ A Miracle Cure ❧

(1883)

Elmira, N.Y., August 1, 1883.

To the Magnetic Rock Spring Company:

Dear Sirs:—I find the following in your advertising pamphlet:

"Our Magnetic Rock Spring is 335 feet deep, and has a flow of 5,000 gallons in twenty-four hours."

I note this paragraph, also:

"Our Magnetic Rock Spring Water cures Rheumatism, Dyspepsia, Liver Complaint, Constipation, Dropsy, Paralysis, St. Vitus' Dance, Delirium Tremens, Diabetes, Stone in the Bladder, Blood Diseases, Scrofula, Ulcers, Female Weakness and General Debility."

I do believe that is what is the matter with me. It reads just like my symptoms. Therefore, please send me, with bill, one barrel of your Magnetic Water, and if I like it I will take the rest.

Also, please instruct me as to dose—for adult. Also, what do you put with it? I mean, what do you put with it to divert your mind from observing that you are taking medicine? Will it go with temperance beverages! I mean, soda water, lemonade, panada, milk, whisky, and such things. I am thus strict because I am a Grandson of Temperance, my father having been a Son of Temperance. Temperance is deeply imbedded in our family. It is for this reason that I ask, and repeat, will it go with temperance beverages?—will it go with the moistures I have mentioned? If with whisky, what portion of the water is best, combined with what disproportion of whisky?—for an adult, as remarked before.

Yours, in alert expectancy.

Mark Twain

P. S. The order is genuine, anyway. The rest of the screed—now that I come to read it over—appears to wander from the point, in places.

## ❧ Experience of the McWilliamses with Membranous Croup ☙

(1875)

[*As related to the author of this book by Mr. McWilliams, a pleasant New York gentleman whom the said author met by chance on a journey.*]

Well, to go back to where I was before I digressed to explain to you how that frightful and incurable disease, membranous croup, was ravaging the town and driving all mothers mad with terror, I called Mrs. McWilliams's attention to little Penelope and said:

"Darling, I wouldn't let that child be chewing that pine stick if I were you."

"Precious, where is the harm in it?" said she, but at the same time preparing to take away the stick—for women cannot receive even the most palpably judicious suggestion without arguing it; that is, married women.

I replied:

"Love, it is notorious that pine is the least nutritious wood that a child can eat."

My wife's hand paused, in the act of taking the stick, and returned itself to her lap. She bridled perceptibly, and said:

"Hubby, you know better than that. You know you do. Doctors *all* say that the turpentine in pine wood is good for weak back and the kidneys."

"Ah—I was under a misapprehension. I did not know that the child's kidneys and spine were affected, and that the family physician had recommended—"

"Who said the child's spine and kidneys were affected?"

"My love, you intimated it."

"The idea! I never intimated anything of the kind."

"Why my dear, it hasn't been two minutes since you said—"

"Bother what I said! I don't care what I did say. There isn't any harm in the child's chewing a bit of pine stick if she wants to, and you know it perfectly well. And she *shall* chew it, too. So there, now!"

"Say no more, my dear. I now see the force of your reasoning, and I will go and order two or three cords of the best pine wood to-day. No child of mine shall want while I—"

"*O please* go along to your office and let me have some peace. A body can never make the simplest remark but you must take it up and go to arguing and arguing and arguing till you don't know what you are talking about, and you *never* do."

"Very well, it shall be as you say. But there is a want of logic in your last remark which—"

However, she was gone with a flourish before I could finish, and had taken the child with her. That night at dinner she confronted me with a face as white as a sheet:

"O, Mortimer, there's another! Little Georgie Gordon is taken."

"Membranous croup?"

"Membranous croup."

"Is there any hope for him?"

"None in the wide world. O, what is to become of us!"

By and by a nurse brought in our Penelope to say good-night and offer the customary prayer at the mother's knee. In the midst of "Now I lay me down to sleep," she gave a slight cough! My wife fell back like one stricken with death. But the next moment she was up and brimming with the activities which terror inspires.

She commanded that the child's crib be removed from the nursery to our bed-room; and she went along to see the order executed. She took me with her, of course. We got matters arranged with speed. A cot bed was put up in my wife's dressing room for the nurse. But now Mrs. McWilliams said we were too far away from the other baby, and what if *he* were to have the symptoms in the night—and she blanched again, poor thing.

We then restored the crib and the nurse to the nursery and put up a bed for ourselves in a room adjoining.

Presently, however, Mrs. McWilliams said suppose the baby should catch it from Penelope? This thought struck a new panic to her heart, and the tribe of us could not get the crib out of the nursery again fast enough to satisfy my wife, though she assisted in her own person and well nigh pulled the crib to pieces in her frantic hurry.

We moved down stairs; but there was no place there to stow the nurse, and Mrs. McWilliams said the nurse's experience would be an inestimable help. So we returned, bag and baggage, to our own bed-room once more, and felt a great gladness, like storm-buffeted birds that have found their nest again.

Mrs. McWilliams sped to the nursery to see how things were going on there. She was back in a moment with a new dread. She said:

"What *can* make Baby sleep so?"

I said:

"Why, my darling, Baby *always* sleeps like a graven image."

"I know. I know; but there's something peculiar about his sleep, now. He seems to—to—he seems to breathe so *regularly*. O, this is dreadful."

"But my dear he always breathes regularly."

"Oh, I know it, but there's something frightful about it now. His nurse is too young and inexperienced. Maria shall stay there with her, and be on hand if anything happens."

"That is a good idea, but who will help *you?*"

"You can help me all I want. I wouldn't allow anybody to do anything but myself, any how, at such a time as this."

I said I would feel mean to lie abed and sleep, and leave her to watch and toil over our little patient all the weary night. But she reconciled me to it. So old Maria departed and took up her ancient quarters in the nursery.

Penelope coughed twice in her sleep.

"Oh, why *don't* that doctor come! Mortimer, this room is too warm. This room is certainly too warm. Turn off the register—quick!"

I shut it off, glancing at the thermometer at the same time, and wondering to myself if 70 *was* too warm for a sick child.

The coachman arrived from down town, now, with the news that our physician was ill and confined to his bed. Mrs. McWilliams turned a dead eye upon me, and said in a dead voice:

"There is a Providence in it. It is foreordained. He never was sick before. Never. We have not been living as we ought to live, Mortimer. Time and time again I have told you so. Now you see the result. Our child will never get well. Be thankful if you can forgive yourself; I never can forgive *my*self."

I said, without intent to hurt, but with heedless choice of words, that I could not see that we had been living such an abandoned life.

"*Mortimer!* Do you want to bring the judgment upon Baby, too!"

Then she began to cry, but suddenly exclaimed:

"The doctor must have sent medicines!"

I said:

"Certainly. They are here. I was only waiting for you to give me a chance."

"Well do give them to me! Don't you know that every moment is precious now? But what was the use in sending medicines, when he *knows* that the disease is incurable?"

I said that while there was life there was hope.

"Hope! Mortimer, you know no more what you are talking about than the child unborn. If you would—. As I live, the directions say give one teaspoonful once an hour! Once an hour!—as if we had a whole year before us to save the child in! Mortimer, please hurry. Give the poor perishing thing a table-spoonful, and *try* to be quick!"

"Why, my dear, a table-spoonful might—"

"*Don't* drive me frantic! . . . . . There, there, there, my precious, my own; it's nasty bitter stuff, but it's good for Nelly—good for mother's precious darling; and it will make her well. There, there, there, put the little head on Mamma's breast and go to sleep, and pretty soon—Oh, I know she can't live till morning! Mortimer, a table-spoonful every half hour will—. Oh, the child needs belladonna too; I know she does—and aconite. Get them, Mortimer. Now do let me have my way. You know nothing about these things."

We now went to bed, placing the crib close to my wife's pillow. All this turmoil had worn upon me, and within two minutes I was something more than half asleep. Mrs. McWilliams roused me:

"Darling, is that register turned on?"

"No."

"I thought as much. Please turn it on at once. This room is cold."

I turned it on, and presently fell asleep again. I was aroused once more:

"Dearie, would you mind moving the crib to your side of the bed? It is nearer the register."

I moved it, but had a collision with the rug and woke up the child. I dozed off once more, while my wife quieted the sufferer. But in a little while these words came murmuring remotely through the fog of my drowsiness:

"Mortimer, if we only had some goose-grease—will you ring?"

I climbed dreamily out, and stepped on a cat, which responded with a protest and would have got a convincing kick for it if a chair had not got it instead.

"Now, Mortimer, why do you want to turn up the gas and wake up the child again?"

"Because I want to see how much I am hurt, Caroline."

"Well look at the chair, too—I have no doubt it is ruined. Poor cat, suppose you had—"

"Now I am not going to suppose anything about the cat. It never would have occurred if Maria had been allowed to remain here and attend to these duties, which are in her line and are not in mine."

"Now Mortimer, I should think you would be ashamed to make a remark like that. It is a pity if you cannot do the few little things I ask of you at such an awful time as this when our child—"

"There, there, I will do anything you want. But I can't raise anybody with this bell. They're all gone to bed. Where is the goose-grease?"

"On the mantel piece in the nursery. If you'll step there and speak to Maria—"

I fetched the goose-grease and went to sleep again. Once more I was called:

"Mortimer, I so hate to disturb you, but the room is still too cold for me to try to apply this stuff. Would you mind lighting the fire? It is all ready to touch a match to."

I dragged myself out and lit the fire, and then sat down disconsolate.

"Mortimer, don't sit there and catch your death of cold. Come to bed."

As I was stepping in, she said:

"But wait a moment. Please give the child some more of the medicine."

Which I did. It was a medicine which made a child more or less lively; so my wife made use of its waking interval to strip it and grease it all over with the goose-oil. I was soon asleep once more, but once more I had to get up.

"Mortimer, I feel a draft. I feel it distinctly. There is nothing so bad for this disease as a draft. Please move the crib in front of the fire."

I did it; and collided with the rug again, which I threw in the fire. Mrs. McWilliams sprang out of bed and rescued it and we had some words. I had another trifling interval of sleep, and then got up, by request, and constructed a flax-seed poultice. This was placed upon the child's breast and left there to do its healing work.

A wood fire is not a permanent thing. I got up every twenty minutes and renewed ours, and this gave Mrs. McWilliams the opportunity to shorten the times of giving the medicines by ten minutes, which was a great satisfaction to her. Now and then, between times, I reorganized the flax-seed poultices, and applied sinapisms and other sorts of blisters where unoccupied places could be found upon the child. Well, toward morning the wood gave out and my wife wanted me to go down cellar and get some more. I said:

"My dear, it is a laborious job, and the child must be nearly warm enough, with her extra clothing. Now mightn't we put on another layer of poultices and—"

I did not finish, because I was interrupted. I lugged wood up from below for some little time, and then turned in and fell to snoring as only a man can whose strength is all gone and whose soul is worn out. Just at broad daylight I felt a grip on my shoulder that brought me to my senses suddenly. My wife was glaring down upon me and gasping. As soon as she could command her tongue she said:

"It is all over! All over! The child's perspiring! What *shall* we do?"

"Mercy, how you terrify me! *I* don't know what we ought to do. Maybe if we scraped her and put her in the draft again—"

"O, idiot! There is not a moment to lose! Go for the doctor. Go yourself. Tell him he *must* come, dead or alive."

I dragged that poor sick man from his bed and brought him. He looked at the child and said she was not dying. This was joy unspeakable to me, but it made my wife as mad as if he had offered her a personal affront. Then he said the child's cough was only caused by some trifling irritation or other in the throat. At this I thought my wife had a mind to show him the door. Now the doctor said he would make the child cough harder and dislodge the trouble. So he gave her something that sent her into a spasm of coughing, and presently up came a little wood splinter or so.

"This child has no membranous croup," said he. "She has been chewing a bit of pine shingle or something of the kind, and got some little slivers in her throat. They won't do her any hurt."

"No," said I, "I can well believe that. Indeed the turpentine that is in them is very good for certain sorts of diseases that are peculiar to children. My wife will tell you so."

But she did not. She turned away in disdain and left the room; and since that time there is one episode in our life which we never refer to. Hence the tide of our days flows by in deep and untroubled serenity.

[Very few married men have such an experience as McWilliams's, and so the author of this book thought that maybe the novelty of it would give it a passing interest to the reader.]

##  Smoking, Diet, and Health at Age Seventy

(from a 1905 speech)

The seventieth birthday! It is the time of life when you arrive at a new and awful dignity; when you may throw aside the decent reserves which have oppressed you for a generation and stand unafraid and unabashed upon your seven-terraced summit and look down and teach—unrebuked. You can tell the world how you got there. It is what they all do. You shall never get tired of telling by what delicate arts and deep moralities you climbed up to that great place. You will explain the process and dwell on the particulars with senile rapture. I have been anxious to explain my own system this long time, and now at last I have the right.

I have achieved my seventy years in the usual way: by sticking strictly to a scheme of life which would kill anybody else. It sounds like an exaggeration, but that is really the common rule for attaining to old age. When we examine the programme of any of these garrulous old people we always find that the habits which have preserved them would have decayed us; that the way of life which enabled them to live upon the property of their heirs so long, as Mr. Choate says, would have put us out of commission ahead of time. I will offer here, as a sound maxim, this: That we can't reach old age by another man's road.

I will now teach, offering my way of life to whomsoever desires to commit suicide by the scheme which has enabled me to beat the doctor and the hangman for seventy years. Some of the details may sound untrue, but they are not. I am not here to deceive; I am here to teach.

We have no permanent habits until we are forty. Then they begin to harden, presently they petrify, then business begins. Since forty I have been regular about going to bed and getting up—and that is one of the main things. I have made it a rule to go to bed when there wasn't anybody left to sit up with; and I have made it a rule to get up when I had to. This has resulted in an unswerving regularity of irregularity. It has saved me sound, but it would injure another person.

In the matter of diet—which is another main thing—I have been persistently strict in sticking to the things which didn't agree with me until one or the other of us got the best of it. Until lately I got the best of it myself. But

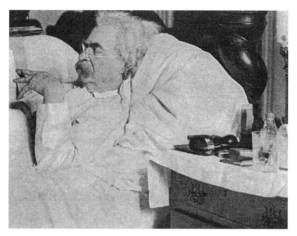

In his later years, Mark Twain often did his writing in bed, with pipe
and cigar at hand, and welcomed interviewers and photographers there. In this
1906 photo taken by Arthur Brown at Mark Twain's home at 21 Fifth Avenue in
New York City, an optical illusion suggests that a fair-haired child is whispering
in the author's ear. *Harper's Weekly* outlined the false image for its readers
in its 8 December 1906 issue.

last spring I stopped frolicking with mince-pie after midnight; up to then I had always believed it wasn't loaded. For thirty years I have taken coffee and bread at eight in the morning, and no bite nor sup until seven-thirty in the evening. Eleven hours. That is all right for me, and is wholesome, because I have never had a headache in my life, but headachy people would not reach seventy comfortably by that road, and they would be foolish to try it. And I wish to urge upon you this—which I think is wisdom—that if you find you can't make seventy by any but an uncomfortable road, don't you go. When they take off the Pullman and retire you to the rancid smoker, put on your things, count your checks, and get out at the first way station where there's a cemetery.

I have made it a rule never to smoke more than one cigar at a time. I have no other restriction as regards smoking. I do not know just when I began to smoke, I only know that it was in my father's lifetime, and that I was discreet. He passed from this life early in 1847, when I was a shade past eleven; ever since then I have smoked publicly. As an example to others, and not that I care for moderation myself, it has always been my rule never to smoke when asleep, and never to refrain when awake. It is a good rule. I mean, for me; but some of you know quite well that it wouldn't answer for everybody that's trying to get to be seventy.

I smoke in bed until I have to go to sleep; I wake up in the night, sometimes once, sometimes twice, sometimes three times, and I never waste any of these opportunities to smoke. This habit is so old and dear and precious to me that if I should break it I should feel as you, sir, would feel if you should lose the only moral you've got—meaning the chairman—if you've got one: I am making no charges. I will grant, here, that I have stopped smoking now and then, for a few months at a time, but it was not on principle, it was only to show off; it was to pulverize those critics who said I was a slave to my habits and couldn't break my bonds.

To-day it is all of sixty years since I began to smoke the limit. I have never bought cigars with life-belts around them. I early found that those were too expensive for me. I have always bought cheap cigars—reasonably cheap, at any rate. Sixty years ago they cost me four dollars a barrel, but my taste has improved, latterly, and I pay seven now. Six or seven. Seven, I think. Yes, it's seven. But that includes the barrel. I often have smoking-parties at my house; but the people that come have always just taken the pledge. I wonder why that is?

As for drinking, I have no rule about that. When the others drink I like to help; otherwise I remain dry, by habit and preference. This dryness does not hurt me, but it could easily hurt you, because you are different. You let it alone.

Since I was seven years old I have seldom taken a dose of medicine, and have still seldomer needed one. But up to seven I lived exclusively on allopathic medicines. Not that I needed them, for I don't think I did; it was for economy; my father took a drug-store for a debt, and it made cod-liver oil cheaper than the other breakfast foods. We had nine barrels of it, and it lasted me seven years. Then I was weaned. The rest of the family had to get along with rhubarb and ipecac and such things, because I was the pet. I was the first Standard Oil Trust. I had it all. By the time the drug-store was exhausted my health was established, and there has never been much the matter with me since. But you know very well it would be foolish for the average child to start for seventy on that basis. It happened to be just the thing for me, but that was merely an accident; it couldn't happen again in a century.

I have never taken any exercise, except sleeping and resting, and I never intend to take any. Exercise is loathsome. And it cannot be any benefit when you are tired; and I was always tired. But let another person try my way, and see where he will come out.

I desire now to repeat and emphasize that maxim: We can't reach old age by another man's road. My habits protect my life, but they would assassinate you.

# ⚜ Parenting and the Ethical Child ⚜

*Mark Twain was a persuasive and original moralist deeply
interested in the development of conscience in childhood. His observations
as a parent confirmed his respect for the intuitive ethical nature of children
and for their frankness and pragmatism. At the same time, he flirted
with an entirely opposite theory: the suspicion that morality
was merely the product of convention and education.*

→ The most permanent lessons in morals are
   those which come, not of booky teaching,
   but of experience.

→ It is a shameful thing to insult a little child.
   It has its feelings, it has its small dignity;
   and since it cannot defend them, it is surely
   an ignoble act to injure them.

#  The Late Benjamin Franklin

(1870)

[Never put off till to-morrow what you can do day after to-morrow just as well.—B. F.]

This party was one of those persons whom they call Philosophers. He was twins, being born simultaneously in two different houses in the city of Boston. These houses remain unto this day, and have signs upon them worded in accordance with the facts. The signs are considered well enough to have, though not necessary, because the inhabitants point out the two birth-places to the stranger anyhow, and sometimes as often as several times in the same day. The subject of this memoir was of a vicious disposition, and early prostituted his talents to the invention of maxims and aphorisms calculated to inflict suffering upon the rising generation of all subsequent ages. His simplest acts, also, were contrived with a view to their being held up for the emulation of boys forever—boys who might otherwise have been happy. It was in this spirit that he became the son of a soap-boiler; and probably for no other reason than that the efforts of all future boys who tried to be anything might be looked upon with suspicion unless they were the sons of soap-boilers. With a malevolence which is without parallel in history, he would work all day and then sit up nights and let on to be studying algebra by the light of a smouldering fire, so that all other boys might have to do that also or else have Benjamin Franklin thrown up to them. Not satisfied with these proceedings, he had a fashion of living wholly on bread and water, and studying astronomy at meal time—a thing which has brought affliction to millions of boys since, whose fathers had read Franklin's pernicious biography.

His maxims were full of animosity toward boys. Nowadays a boy cannot follow out a single natural instinct without tumbling over some of those everlasting aphorisms and hearing from Franklin on the spot. If he buys two cents' worth of peanuts, his father says, "Remember what Franklin has said, my son,—'A groat a day's a penny a year;'" and the comfort is all gone out of those peanuts. If he wants to spin his top when he is done work, his father quotes, "Procrastination is the thief of time." If he does a virtuous action, he never gets anything for it, because "Virtue is its own reward." And that boy is hounded to death and robbed of his natural rest, because Franklin said once in one of his inspired flights of malignity—

> Early to bed and early to rise
> Make a man healthy and wealthy and wise.

As if it were any object to a boy to be healthy and wealthy and wise on such terms. The sorrow that that maxim has cost me through my parents' experimenting on me with it, tongue cannot tell. The legitimate result is my present state of general debility, indigence, and mental aberration. My parents used to have me up before nine o'clock in the morning, sometimes, when I was a boy. If they had let me take my natural rest, where would I have been now? Keeping store, no doubt, and respected by all.

And what an adroit old adventurer the subject of this memoir was! In order to get a chance to fly his kite on Sunday, he used to hang a key on the string and let on to be fishing for lightning. And a guileless public would go home chirping about the "wisdom" and the "genius" of the hoary Sabbath-breaker. If anybody caught him playing "mumble-peg" by himself, after the age of sixty, he would immediately appear to be ciphering out how the grass grew—as if it was any of his business. My grandfather knew him well, and he says Franklin was always fixed—always ready. If a body, during his old age, happened on him unexpectedly when he was catching flies, or making mud pies, or sliding on a cellar-door, he would immediately look wise, and rip out a maxim, and walk off with his nose in the air and his cap turned wrong side before, trying to appear absent-minded and eccentric. He was a hard lot.

He invented a stove that would smoke your head off in four hours by the clock. One can see the almost devilish satisfaction he took in it, by his giving it his name.

He was always proud of telling how he entered Philadelphia, for the first time, with nothing in the world but two shillings in his pocket and four rolls of bread under his arm. But really, when you come to examine it critically, it was nothing. Anybody could have done it.

To the subject of this memoir belongs the honor of recommending the army to go back to bows and arrows in place of bayonets and muskets. He observed, with his customary force, that the bayonet was very well, under some circumstances, but that he doubted whether it could be used with accuracy at long range.

Benjamin Franklin did a great many notable things for his country, and made her young name to be honored in many lands as the mother of such a son. It is not the idea of this memoir to ignore that or cover it up. No; the simple idea of it is to snub those pretentious maxims of his, which he worked up with a great show of originality out of truisms that had become wearisome platitudes as early as the dispersion from Babel; and also to snub his stove, and his military inspirations, his unseemly endeavor to make himself conspicuous when he entered Philadelphia, and his flying his kite and fooling away his time in all sorts of such ways, when he ought to have been foraging for soap-fat, or constructing candles. I merely desire to do away with somewhat of the prevalent calamitous idea among heads of families that Franklin *acquired* his great genius by working for nothing, studying by moonlight, and getting up in the night instead of waiting till morning like a Christian, and that this programme, rigidly inflicted, will make a Franklin of every father's fool. It is time these gentlemen were finding out that these execrable eccentricities of instinct and conduct are only the *evidences* of genius, not the *creators* of it. I wish I had been the father of my parents long enough to make them comprehend this truth, and thus prepare them to let their son have an easier time of it. When I was a child I had to boil soap, notwithstanding my father was wealthy, and I had to get up early and study geometry at breakfast, and peddle my own poetry, and do everything just as Franklin did, in the solemn hope that I would be a Franklin some day. And here I am.

## On Theft and Conscience

(from a 1902 speech)

I have seen it stated in print that as a boy I had been guilty of stealing peaches, apples, and watermelons. I read a story to this effect very closely not long ago, and I was convinced of one thing, which was that the man who wrote it was of the opinion that it was wrong to steal, and that I had not acted right in doing so. I wish now, however, to make an honest statement, which is that I do not believe, in all my checkered career, I stole a ton of peaches.

One night I stole—I mean I removed—a watermelon from a wagon while the owner was attending to another customer. I crawled off to a secluded spot, where I found that it was green. It was the greenest melon in the Mississippi Valley. Then I began to reflect. I began to be sorry. I wondered what George Washington would have done had he been in my place. I thought a long time, and then suddenly felt that strange feeling which comes to a man with a good resolution, and took up that watermelon and took it back to its owner. I handed him the watermelon and told him to reform. He took my lecture much to heart, and, when he gave me a good one in place of the green melon, I forgave him.

I told him that I would still be a customer of his, and that I cherished no ill-feeling because of the incident—that would remain green in my memory.

##  On Training Children

(from "A Family Sketch," 1906)

Conscious teaching is good and necessary, and in a hundred instances it effects its purpose, while in a hundred others it fails and the purpose, if accomplished at all, is accomplished by some other agent or influence. I suppose that in most cases changes take place in us without our being aware of it at the time, and in after life we give the credit of it—if it be of a creditable nature—to mamma, or the school or the pulpit. But I know of one case where a change was wrought in me by an outside influence—where teaching had failed,—and I was profoundly aware of the change when it happened. And so I know that the fact that for more than fifty-five years I have not wantonly injured a dumb creature is not to be credited to home, school or pulpit, but to a momentary outside influence. When I was a boy my mother pleaded for the fishes and the birds and tried to persuade me to spare them, but I went on taking their lives unmoved, until at last I shot a bird that sat in a high tree, with its head tilted back, and pouring out a grateful song from an innocent heart. It toppled from its perch and came floating down limp and forlorn and fell at my feet, its song quenched and its unoffending life extinguished. I had not needed that harmless creature,

I had destroyed it wantonly, and I felt all that an assassin feels, of grief and remorse when his deed comes home to him and he wishes he could undo it and have his hands and his soul clean again from accusing blood. One department of my education, theretofore long and diligently and fruitlessly labored upon, was closed by that single application of an outside and unsalaried influence, and could take down its sign and put away its books and its admonitions permanently.

In my turn I admonished the children not to hurt animals; also to protect weak animals from stronger ones. This teaching succeeded—and not only in the spirit but in the letter. When Clara was small—small enough to wear a shoe the size of a cowslip—she suddenly brought this shoe down with determined energy, one day, dragged it rearward with an emphatic rake, then stooped down to examine results. We inquired, and she explained—

"The naughty big ant was trying to kill the little one!"

Neither of them survived the generous interference.

The schoolroom in the Clemenses' Hartford house.
(Courtesy of the Mark Twain House, Hartford, Conn.)

# ❧ A Sampling of Childish Ethics ❧

(selections from a manuscript compiled between 1876 and 1885
about Clemens's daughters, Susy, Clara ["Bay"], and Jean)

One day on the ombra Susie burst into song, as follows:

"O Jesus are you dead, so you cannot dance and sing!"

The air was exceedingly gay—rather pretty, too—and was accompanied by
a manner and gestures that were equally gay and chipper. Her mother was astonished and distressed. She said:

"Why Susie! Did Maria teach you that dreadful song?"

"No, mamma, I made it myself all out of my own head. *No*-body helped me."

She was plainly proud of it, and went on repeating it with great content.

[Maria McLaughlin was one of Clara Clemens's innumerable wet nurses—
a profane devil, and given to whisky, tobacco, and some of the vices.]

————

About a fortnight ago Bay got what may be called about her first thrashing.
Her mother took both children gravely to the bedchamber to punish them. It
was all new to Bay and the novelty of it charmed her. Madam turned Susie across
her lap and began to spat her (very lightly). Bay was delighted with the episode.
Then *she* was called for, and came skipping forward with jovial alacrity and
threw herself across her mother's lap as who should say, "My, but ain't these
good times!" The spat descended sharply, and by the war-whoop that followed,
one perceived that the Bay's ideas about these festivities had changed. The
madam could not whip for laughing and had to leave the punishment but half
performed.

Olivia Susan (Susy) Clemens (1872–96) in 1878 and in 1890 or 1891
during her brief attendance at Bryn Mawr College in Pennsylvania.
(Courtesy of the Mark Twain House, Hartford, Conn.)

---

Susie—4½. Perceiving that her shoes were damaging her feet, from being too small, I got her a very ample pair, of a most villainous shape and style. She made no complaint when they were put on her, but looked injured and degraded. At night when she knelt at her mother's knee to say her prayers, the former gave her the usual admonition:

"Now, Susie—think about God."

"Mamma, I can't, with these shoes."

---

October, 1876 (aged 4 and upwards).—Susie's mother read to her the story of Joseph. The killing of the kid to stain the garment with blood was arrived at, in due course and made a deep impression. Susie's comment, full of sympathy and compassion, was: "*Poor little kid!*" This is probably the only time, in 4000 years, that any human being has pitied that kid—everybody has been too much taken up with pitying Joseph, to remember that that innocent little animal suffered even more violently than he, and is fairly entitled to a word of compassion. I did not suppose that an unhackneyed (let alone an original) thought could be started on an Old Bible subject, but plainly this is one.

————

Susie has always had a good deal of womanly dignity. One day Livy and Mrs. Lilly Warner were talking earnestly in the library; Susie interrupted them several times; finally Livy said, very sharply, "Susie, if you interrupt again, I will send you instantly to the nursery!" Five minutes later, Livy saw Mrs. W. to the front door; on her way back she saw Susie on the stairs, and said, "Where are you going, Susie?" "To the nursery, mamma." "What are you going up there, for, dear?—don't you want to stay with me in the library?" "You didn't speak to me *right*, mamma." Livy was surprised; she had forgotten that rebuke; she pushed her inquiries further; Susie said, with a gentle dignity that carried its own reproach, "You didn't speak to me *right*, mamma." She had been humiliated in the presence of an outsider. Livy felt condemned. She carried Susie to the library, and argued the case with her. Susie hadn't a fault to find with the justice of the rebuke, but she held out steadily against the *manner* of it, saying gently, once or twice, "But you didn't speak to me *right*, mamma." She won her cause; and her mother had to confess that she *had*n't spoken to her "right."

We require courteous speech from the children at all times and in all circumstances; we owe them the same courtesy in return; and when we fail of it we deserve correction.

One day Livy and Clara Spaulding were exclaiming over the odd, queer ways of the French. Susie looked up from her work of doll-dressing and said, "Well, mamma, don't you reckon we seem queer to *them?*"

———

She is growing steadily into an admirably discriminating habit of language. Yes, and into the use of pretty large words, too, sometimes—as witness: The night before, I referred to some preference expressed by Jean. Susie wanted at once to know *how* she expressed it—inasmuch as Jean knows only about a dozen words. I said, "Why she spoke up, with marked asperity, and exclaimed, 'Well, Mr. Clemens, you may support that fallacy, if native perversity and a fatuous imagination so move you; but the exact opposite is my distinct and decided preference.'"

Susie's grave eyes stood wide open during this speech; she was silent a moment to let it soak home, then said in a tone of absolute conviction, "Well, papa, that *is* an exaggeration!"

———

One evening Susie had prayed; Bay was curled up for sleep; she was reminded that it was her turn to pray, now; she said, "O, one's enough!" and dropped off to slumber.

———

Once in Paris we found that Susie had about ceased from praying. The matter was inquired into. She answered, with simplicity: "I hardly ever pray, now; when I want anything, I just leave it to Him—He understands."

[The words, without her voice and manner, do not convey her meaning. What she meant, was, that she had thought the thing all out, and arrived at the conclusion that there was no obstructing vagueness or confusion between herself and God requiring her to explain herself in set words;—when she felt a want, He knew it without its being formulated, and could be trusted to grant or wisely withhold as should be best for both parties; and she was conscious of the impropriety and the needlessness of bothering Him with every little craving that came into her head.]

———

I wish I could recal some of Susie's speeches which illustrate her discriminating *exactness* in the matter of expressing herself upon difficult and elusive points, for they have often been remarkable—some of them were as good, in the matter of discriminating between fine shades of meaning, as any grown person could turn out.

Even Bay is beginning to avoid looseness of statement, now, and to lean toward an almost hypercritical exactness. The other day she was about to start on an excursion among the calves and chickens in the back enclosure, when her Aunt Sue, feeling compassion for her loneliness, proposed to go with her. Bay showed a gratification of so composed a nature that it was hard to tell it from indifference, with the naked eye. So aunt Sue added—"That is, if you would be happier to have me go——would you be happier?" Bay turned the thing over in her mind a couple of times, to make sure, then said, "Well—I should be *happy*, but not HAPPIER."

One couldn't ask to have a thing trimmed any finer than that, I think.

———

Clara picked up a book—"Daniel Boone, by John S. C. Abbott" and found on the fly-leaf a comment of mine, in pencil; puzzled over it, couldn't quite make it out; her mother took it and read it to her, as follows: "A poor slovenly book; a mess of sappy drivel and bad grammar." Clara said, with entire seriousness

Clara Langdon Clemens (later Gabrilowitsch, then Samossoud;
1874–1962) in 1878 and in 1929. (1878 photo courtesy of the
Mark Twain House, Hartford, Conn.)

(not comprehending the meaning but charmed with the sound of the words,)
"O, that must be lovely!" and carried the book away and buried herself in it.

———————

I stepped into the nursery on my way to the billiard room after breakfast. I
had a newspaper-cutting in my hand, just received in the mail, and its spirit
was upon me—the spirit of funerals and gloom. Jean sat playing on the floor,
the incandescent core of a conflagration of flooding sunlight—and she and
her sunny splendors were suggestive of just the opposite spirit. She said, with
great interest,—

Jane Lampton (Jean) Clemens (1880–1909) in 1884 and
in 1909. (1909 photo courtesy of the Mark Twain
House, Hartford, Conn.)

"What is it in the little piece of paper you got in yo' hand, papa—what do
it say?"

I said, impressively, and meaning to impress *her*, —

"It tells about an old, old friend of mine, Jean—friend away back yonder
years and years and years ago, when I was young—very dear friend, and now
he is dead, Jean."

She uttered an ejaculation and I a response.

Then she looked earnestly up from down there, and said,—

"Is he gone up in heaven, papa?"

"Yes," I said, "he is gone up in heaven."

A reflective pause—then she said,—

"Was he down on the earth, papa—down here?"

"Yes, he was down here on the earth, where we are."

She lowered her face, now grown very grave, and reflected again, two or three moments. Then she lifted it quickly to mine, and inquired with a burning interest,—

"And did along comed a blackbird and nipped off his nose?"

The solemnity of the occasion was gone to the devil in a moment—as far as I was concerned; though Jean was not aware that *she* had done anything toward that result. She was asking simply and solely for information, and was not intending to be lightsome or frivolous.

————

Mention was made of a certain young lady, at breakfast; and Susie remarked that she was very pretty. Her mother said no, she had a good face, a face which answered to her exceptionally fine character, but she would hardly call it a pretty face. Susie said—

"But mama, I think that when a person has a good figure and a pleasant face that one likes to look at, she *is* pretty."

Rev. Thos. K. Beecher was present, and said it was a nice distinction, and that Susie's position was sound.

# Youthful Misdemeanors

(from a 1902 speech)

In that old time it was a paradise for simplicity—it was a simple, simple life, cheap but comfortable, and full of sweetness, and there was nothing of this rage of modern civilization there at all. It was a delectable land. I went out there last June, and I met in that town of Hannibal a schoolmate of mine, John Briggs, whom I had not seen for more than fifty years. I tell you, that was a meeting! That pal whom I had known as a little boy long ago, and knew now as a stately man three or four inches over six feet and browned by exposure to many climes, he was back there to see that old place again. We spent a whole afternoon going about here and there and yonder, and hunting up the scenes and talking of the crimes which we had committed so long ago. It was a heart-breaking delight, full of pathos, laughter, and tears, all mixed together; and we called the roll of the boys and girls that we picnicked and sweethearted with so many years ago, and there were hardly half a dozen of them left; the rest were in their graves; and we went up there on the summit of that hill, a treasured place in my memory, the summit of Holliday's Hill, and looked out again over that magnificent panorama of the Mississippi River, sweeping along league after league, a level green paradise on one side, and retreating capes and promontories as far as you could see on the other, fading away in the soft, rich lights of the remote distance. I recognized then that I was seeing now the most enchanting river view the planet could furnish. I never knew it when I was a boy; it took an educated eye that had travelled over the globe to know and appreciate it; and John said, "Can you point out the place where Bear Creek used to be before the railroad came?" I said, "Yes, it ran along yonder." "And can you point out the swimming-hole?" "Yes, out there." And he said, "Can you point out the place where we stole the skiff?" Well, I didn't know which one he meant. Such a wilderness of events had intervened since that day, more than fifty years ago, it took me more than five minutes to call back that little incident, and then I did call it back; it was a white skiff, and we painted it red to allay suspicion. And the saddest, saddest man came along—a stranger he was—and he looked that red skiff over so pathetically, and he said: "Well, if it weren't for the complexion I'd know whose skiff that was." He said it in that pleading way, you know, that appeals for sympathy and suggestion; we were full of sympathy for him, but we weren't in any condition to offer suggestions. I can see him yet as he turned away with that same sad look on his face and vanished out of history forever. I wonder what became of that man. I know what became of the skiff. Well, it was a beautiful life, a lovely life. There was no crime. Merely little things like pillaging orchards and watermelon-patches and breaking the Sabbath—we didn't break the Sabbath often enough to signify—once a week perhaps. But we were good boys, good Presbyterian boys, all Presbyterian boys, and loyal and all that; anyway, we were good Presbyterian boys when the weather was doubtful; when it was fair, we did wander a little from the fold.

## Advice to Youth

(an 1882 speech to a young persons' club)

Being told I would be expected to talk here, I inquired what sort of a talk I ought to make. They said it should be something suitable to youth—something didactic, instructive; or something in the nature of good advice. Very well; I have a few things in my mind which I have often longed to say for the instruction of the young; for it is in one's tender early years that such things will best take root and be most enduring and most valuable. First, then, I will say to you, my young friends—and I say it beseechingly, urgingly—

Always obey your parents, when they are present. This is the best policy in the long run; because if you don't, they will make you. Most parents think they know better than you do; and you can generally make more by humoring that superstition than you can by acting on your own better judgment.

Be respectful to your superiors, if you have any; also to strangers, and sometimes to others. If a person offend you, and you are in doubt as to whether it was intentional or not, do not resort to extreme measures; simply watch your chance and hit him with a brick. That will be sufficient. If you shall find that he had not intended any offense, come out frankly and confess yourself in the wrong when you struck him; acknowledge it like a man, and say you didn't mean to. Yes, always avoid violence; in this age of charity and kindliness, the time has gone by for such things. Leave dynamite to the low and unrefined.

Go to bed early, get up early—this is wise. Some authorities say get up with the sun; some others say get up with one thing, some with another. But a lark is really the best thing to get up with. It gives you a splendid reputation with everybody to know that you get up with the lark; and if you get the right kind of a lark, and work at him right, you can easily train him to get up at half past nine, every time—it is no trick at all.

Now as to the matter of lying. You want to be very careful about lying; otherwise you are nearly sure to get caught. Once caught, you can never again be, in the eyes of the good and the pure, what you were before. Many a young person has injured himself permanently through a single clumsy and ill-finished lie, the result of carelessness born of incomplete training. Some authorities hold that the young ought not to lie at all. That, of course, is putting it rather stronger than necessary; still, while I cannot go quite so far as that, I do maintain, and I believe I am right, that the young ought to be temperate in the use of this great art until practice and experience shall give them that confidence, elegance and precision which alone can make the accomplishment graceful and profitable. Patience, diligence, pains-taking attention to detail—these are the requirements; these, in time, will make the student perfect; upon these, and upon these only, may he rely as the sure foundation for future eminence. Think what tedious years of study, thought, practice, experience, went to the equipment of that peerless old master who was able to impose upon the whole world the lofty and sounding maxim that "Truth is mighty and will prevail,"—the most majestic compound-fracture of fact which any of woman born has yet achieved. For the history of our race, and each individual's experience, are sown thick with evidences that a truth is not hard to kill, and that a lie well told is immortal. There in Boston is a monument to the man who discovered anæsthesia; many people are aware, in these latter days, that that man didn't discover it at all, but stole the discovery from another man. Is this truth mighty, and will it prevail? Ah, no, my hearers, the monument is made of hardy material, but the lie it tells will outlast it a million years. An awkward, feeble, leaky lie is a thing which you ought to make it your unceasing study to avoid; such a lie as that has no more real permanence than an average truth. Why, you might as well tell the truth at once and be done with it. A feeble, stupid, preposterous lie will not live two years—except it be a slander upon somebody. It is indestructible, then, of course, but that is no merit of yours. A final word: begin your practice of this gracious and beautiful art early—begin now. If I had begun earlier, I could have learned how.

Never handle firearms carelessly. The sorrow and suffering that have been caused through the innocent but heedless handling of firearms by the young! Only four days ago, right in the next farm house to the one where I am spending the summer, a mother, old and gray and sweet, one of the loveliest spirits in the land, was sitting at her work, when her young son crept in and got down an old, battered, rusty gun which had not been touched for many years, and was supposed not to be loaded, and pointed it at her, laughing, and threatening to shoot. In her fright she ran screaming and pleading toward the door on the other side of the room; but as she passed him he placed the gun almost against her very breast and pulled the trigger! He had supposed it was not loaded. And he was right: it wasn't. So there wasn't any harm done. It is the only case of the kind I ever heard of. Therefore, just the same, don't you meddle with old unloaded firearms; they are the most deadly and unerring things that have ever been created by man. You don't have to take any pains at all, with them; you don't have to have a rest, you don't have to have any sights on the gun, you don't have to take aim, even. No, you just pick out a relative and bang away, and you are sure to get him. A youth who can't hit a cathedral at thirty yards with a Gatling gun in three quarters of an hour, can take up an old empty musket and bag his mother every time, at a hundred. Think what Waterloo would have been if one of the armies had been boys armed with old rusty muskets supposed not to be loaded, and the other army had been composed of their female relations. The very thought of it makes one shudder.

There are many sorts of books; but good ones are the sort for the young to read: Remember that. They are a great, an inestimable, an unspeakable means of improvement. Therefore be careful in your selection, my young friends; be very careful; confine yourselves exclusively to Robertson's Sermons, Baxter's Saint's Rest, The Innocents Abroad, and works of that kind.

But I have said enough. I hope you will treasure up the instructions which I have given you, and make them a guide to your feet and a light to your understanding. Build your character thoughtfully and pains-takingly upon these precepts; and by and by, when you have got it built, you will be surprised and gratified to see how nicely and sharply it resembles everybody else's.

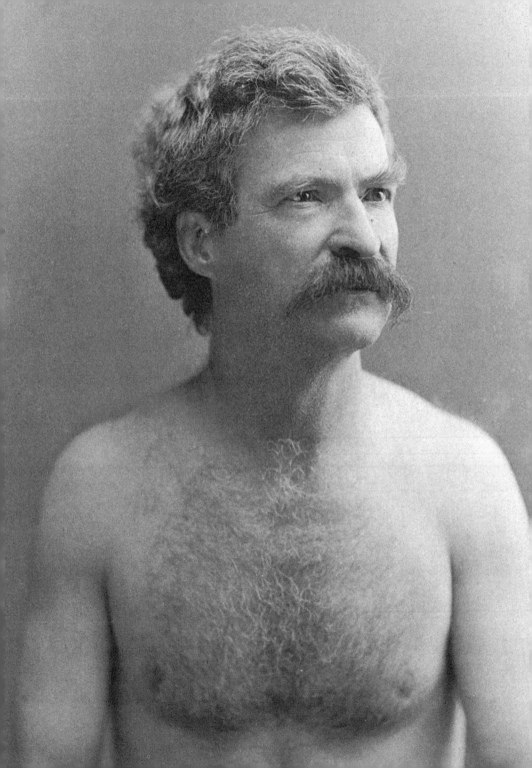

# ❧[ Clothes, Fashion, and Style ]❧

*As a reporter in Nevada in the 1860s, Mark Twain showed an eccentric flair for describing the complexities of female attire. In his own dress, he developed an independent fashion sense, rebelling against the drab and the conventional. "If I had been an ancient Briton," he said in 1907, "I would not have contented myself with blue paint, but I would have bankrupted the rainbow."*

➜ Be careless in your dress if you must, but keep a tidy soul.

➜ Clothes make the man. Naked people have little or no influence in society.

# A Fashion Item

(1868)

At Gen. Grant's reception, the other night, the most fashionably dressed lady was Mrs. G. C. She wore a pink satin dress, plain in front, but with a good deal of rake to it—to the train, I mean; it was said to be two or three yards long. One could see it creeping along the floor some little time after the woman was gone. Mrs. C. wore also a white bodice, cut bias, with Pompadour sleeves, flounced with ruches; low neck, with the inside handkerchief not visible; white kid gloves. She had on a pearl necklace, which glinted lonely, high up in the midst of that barren waste of neck and shoulders. Her hair was frizzled into a tangled chapparal, forward of her ears; aft it was drawn together, and compactly bound and plaited into a stump like a pony's tail, and furthermore was canted upward at a sharp angle, and ingeniously supported by a red velvet crupper, whose forward extremity was made fast with a half hitch around a hairpin on her poop-deck, which means, of course, the top of her head, if you do not understand fashion technicalities. Her whole top-hamper was neat and becoming. She had a beautiful complexion when she first came, but it faded out by degrees in the most unaccountable way. However, it was not lost for good. I found the most of it on my shoulder afterwards. (I had been standing by the door when she had been squeezing in and out with the throng.) There were other fashionably dressed ladies present, of course, but I only took notes of one, as a specimen. The subject is one of great interest to ladies, and I would gladly enlarge upon it if I were more competent to do it justice.

# A FASHION ITEM.

**A**T General G——'s reception the other night, the most fashionably dressed lady was Mrs. G. C. She wore a pink satin dress, plain in front but with a good deal of rake to it—to the train, I mean; it was said to be two or three yards long. One could see it creeping along the floor some little time after the woman was gone. Mrs. C. wore also a white bodice, cut bias, with Pompadour sleeves, flounced with ruches; low neck, with the inside handkerchief not visible, with white kid gloves. She had on a pearl necklace, which glinted lonely, high up the midst of that barren waste of neck and shoulders. Her hair was frizzled into a tangled chapparel, forward of her ears, aft it was drawn together, and compactly bound and plaited into a stump like a pony's tail, and furthermore was canted upward at a sharp angle, and ingeniously supported by a red velvet crupper, whose forward extremity was made fast with a half-hitch around a hairpin on the top of her head. Her whole top hamper was neat and becoming. She had a beautiful complexion when she first came, but it faded out by degrees in an unaccountable way. However, it is not lost for good. I found the most of it on my shoulder afterwards. (I stood near the door when she squeezed out with the throng.) There were other ladies present, but I only took notes of one as a specimen. I would gladly enlarge upon the subject were I able to do it justice.

153

From *Mark Twain's Sketches, New and Old* (1875).

# ❧ The Hand of Fashion ❧

(from *The Innocents Abroad*, 1869)

Every now and then my glove purchase in Gibraltar last night intrudes itself upon me. Dan and the ship's surgeon and I had been up to the great square, listening to the music of the fine military bands, and contemplating English and Spanish female loveliness and fashion, and, at 9 o'clock, were on our way to the theatre, when we met the General, the Judge, the Commodore, the Colonel, and the Commissioner of the United States of America to Europe, Asia, and Africa, who had been to the Club House, to register their several titles and impoverish the bill of fare; and they told us to go over to the little variety store, near the Hall of Justice, and buy some kid gloves. They said they were elegant, and very moderate in price. It seemed a stylish thing to go to the theatre in kid gloves, and we acted upon the hint. A very handsome young lady in the store offered me a pair of blue gloves. I did not want blue, but she said they would look very pretty on a hand like mine. The remark touched me tenderly. I glanced furtively at my hand, and somehow it did seem rather a comely member. I tried a glove on my left, and blushed a little. Manifestly the size was too small for me. But I felt gratified when she said:

"Oh, it is just right!"—yet I knew it was no such thing.

I tugged at it diligently, but it was discouraging work. She said:

"Ah! I see *you* are accustomed to wearing kid gloves—but some gentlemen are *so* awkward about putting them on."

It was the last compliment I had expected. I only understand putting on the buckskin article perfectly. I made another effort, and tore the glove from the base of the thumb into the palm of the hand—and tried to hide the rent. She kept up her compliments, and I kept up my determination to deserve them or die:

"Ah, you have had experience!" [A rip down the back of the hand.] "They are just right for you—your hand is very small—if they tear you need not pay for them." [A rent across the middle.] "I can always tell when a gentleman understands putting on kid gloves. There is a grace about it that only comes with long practice." [The whole after-guard of the glove "fetched away," as the sailors say, the fabric parted across the knuckles, and nothing was left but a melancholy ruin.]

I was too much flattered to make an exposure, and throw the merchandise on the angel's hands. I was hot, vexed, confused, but still happy; but I hated the other boys for taking such an absorbing interest in the proceedings. I wished they were in Jericho. I felt exquisitely mean when I said cheerfully,—

"This one does very well; it fits elegantly. I like a glove that fits. No, never mind, ma'am, never mind; I'll put the other on in the street. It is warm here."

It *was* warm. It was the warmest place I ever was in. I paid the bill, and as I passed out with a fascinating bow, I thought I detected a light in the woman's eye that was gently ironical; and when I looked back from the street, and she was laughing all to herself about something or other, I said to myself, with withering sarcasm, "Oh, certainly; *you* know how to put on kid gloves, don't you?—a self-complacent ass, ready to be flattered out of your senses by every petticoat that chooses to take the trouble to do it!"

The silence of the boys annoyed me. Finally, Dan said, musingly:

"Some gentlemen don't know how to put on kid gloves at all; but some do."

And the doctor said (to the moon, I thought,)

"But it is always easy to tell when a gentleman is used to putting on kid gloves."

Dan soliloquized, after a pause:

"Ah, yes; there is a grace about it that only comes with long, very long practice."

"Yes, indeed, I've noticed that when a man hauls on a kid glove like he was

Mark Twain in his sealskin hat and coat, 1876.
(Courtesy of the Mark Twain House, Hartford, Conn.)

*Clockwise from above:* Mark Twain in London in 1897 (photograph by Alfred Ellis); posing in the basin of a fountain at Stormfield wearing his white suit and fur-lined greatcoat, 1908; in the English countryside in 1900 (courtesy of the Mark Twain House, Hartford, Conn.).

On the beach in Bermuda in 1908.

At Stormfield, about 1908.

dragging a cat out of an ash-hole by the tail, *he* understands putting on kid gloves; *he's* had ex—"

"Boys, enough of a thing's enough! You think you are very smart, I suppose, but I don't. And if you go and tell any of those old gossips in the ship about this thing, I'll never forgive you for it; that's all."

They let me alone then, for the time being. We always let each other alone in time to prevent ill feeling from spoiling a joke. But they had bought gloves, too, as I did. We threw all the purchases away together this morning. They were coarse, unsubstantial, freckled all over with broad yellow splotches, and could neither stand wear nor public exhibition. We had entertained an angel unawares, but we did not take her in. She did that for us.

## That White Suit

(from a 1906 interview)

*Mark Twain's remarks were also reported in the* New York World *of 8 December 1906. His white flannel suit, he explained, was "the uniform of the American Association of Purity and Perfection, of which I am president, secretary and treasurer and the only man in the United States eligible to membership."*

"Why don't you ask why I am wearing such apparently unseasonable clothes? I'll tell you. I have found that when a man reaches the advanced age of 71 years as I have, the continual sight of dark clothing is likely to have a depressing effect upon him. Light-colored clothing is more pleasing to the eye and enlivens the spirit. Now, of course, I cannot compel every one to wear such clothing just for my especial benefit, so I do the next best thing and wear it myself.

"Of course, before a man reaches my years, the fear of criticism might prevent him from indulging his fancy. I am not afraid of that. I am decidedly for pleasing color combinations in dress. I like to see the women's clothes, say, at the opera. What can be more depressing than the sombre black which custom requires men to wear upon state occasions. A group of men in evening clothes looks like a flock of crows, and is just about as inspiring. . . .

"The best-dressed man I have ever seen, however, was a native of the Sandwich Islands, who attracted my attention thirty years ago. Now, when that man wanted to don especial dress to honor a public occasion or a holiday, why he occasionally put on a pair of spectacles. Otherwise the clothing with which God had provided him sufficed."

## Clothes and Deception

(from *Following the Equator*, 1897)

The drive through the town and out to the Galle Face by the seashore, what a dream it was of tropical splendors of bloom and blossom, and Oriental conflagrations of costume! The walking groups of men, women, boys, girls, babies—each individual was a flame, each group a house afire for color. And such stunning colors, such intensely vivid colors, such rich and exquisite minglings and fusings of rainbows and lightnings! And all harmonious, all in perfect taste; never a discordant note; never a color on any person swearing at another color on him or failing to harmonize faultlessly with the colors of any group the wearer might join. The stuffs were silk—thin, soft, delicate, cling-ing; and, as a rule, each piece a solid color: a splendid green, a splendid blue, a splendid yellow, a splendid purple, a splendid ruby, deep, and rich with smoul-dering fires—they swept continuously by in crowds and legions and multi-tudes, glowing, flashing, burning, radiant; and every five seconds came a burst of blinding red that made a body catch his breath, and filled his heart with joy. And then, the unimaginable grace of those costumes! Sometimes a woman's whole dress was but a scarf wound about her person and her head, sometimes a man's was but a turban and a careless rag or two—in both cases generous areas of polished dark skin showing—but always the arrangement compelled the homage of the eye and made the heart sing for gladness.

I can see it to this day, that radiant panorama, that wilderness of rich color, that incomparable dissolving-view of harmonious tints, and lithe half-covered forms, and beautiful brown faces, and gracious and graceful gestures and at-titudes and movements, free, unstudied, barren of stiffness and restraint, and—

Just then, into this dream of fairyland and paradise a grating dissonance was injected. Out of a missionary school came marching, two and two, six-teen prim and pious little Christian black girls, Europeanly clothed—dressed, to the last detail, as they would have been dressed on a summer Sunday in an English or American village. Those clothes—oh, they were unspeakably ugly! Ugly, barbarous, destitute of taste, destitute of grace, repulsive as a shroud. I looked at my women-folk's clothes—just full-grown duplicates of the out-rages disguising those poor little abused creatures—and was ashamed to be seen in the street with them. Then I looked at my own clothes, and was ashamed to be seen in the street with myself.

However, we must put up with our clothes as they are—they have their reason for existing. They are on us to expose us—to advertise what we wear them to conceal. They are a sign; a sign of insincerity; a sign of suppressed vanity; a pretense that we despise gorgeous colors and the graces of harmony and form; and we put them on to propagate that lie and back it up. But we do not deceive our neighbor; and when we step into Ceylon we realize that we have not even deceived ourselves. We do love brilliant colors and graceful costumes; and at home we will turn out in a storm to see them when the procession goes by—and envy the wearers. We go to the theater to look at them and grieve that we can't be clothed like that. We go to the King's ball, when we get a chance, and are glad of a sight of the splendid uniforms and the glittering orders. When we are granted permission to attend an imperial drawing-room we shut ourselves up in private and parade around in the theatrical court-dress by the hour, and admire ourselves in the glass, and are utterly happy; and every member of every governor's staff in democratic America does the same with his grand new uniform—and if he is not watched he will get himself photographed in it, too. When I see the Lord Mayor's footman I am dissatisfied with my lot. Yes, our clothes are a lie, and have been nothing short of that these hundred years. They are insincere, they are the ugly and appropriate outward exposure of an inward sham and a moral decay.

The last little brown boy I chanced to notice in the crowds and swarms of Colombo had nothing on but a twine string around his waist, but in my memory the frank honesty of his costume still stands out in pleasant contrast with the odious flummery in which the little Sunday-school dowdies were masquerading.

#  A Sumptuous Robe

(from a 1908 speech)

*In June 1907 Mark Twain received an honorary doctorate of letters from Oxford University. Several months later, at a dinner in his honor in New York, he delighted his audience by donning his doctoral gown.*

I like the giddy costume. I was born for a savage. There isn't any color that is too bright and too strong for me, and the red—isn't that red? There is no such red as that outside the arteries of an ox. I should just like to wear it all the time, and to go up and down Fifth Avenue and hear the people envy me and wish they dared to wear a costume like that. I am going to a house, to a luncheon party, where there will be nobody present but ladies; I shall be the only lady there of my sex, and I shall put this on and make those ladies look dim.

Mark Twain in his Oxford University cap and gown at his daughter Clara's wedding in October 1909. *Left to right:* Mark Twain, Jervis Langdon II, Jean Clemens, Ossip Gabrilowitsch, Clara Clemens Gabrilowitsch, and the Reverend Joseph H. Twichell.

# ⚜ In Case of Emergency ⚜

---

*In dealing with emergencies, it is useful to remain alert and composed. Sometimes, however, it can be just as important to know when—and how quickly—to retreat. Mark Twain considers the range of appropriate responses to a variety of unexpected situations, from accidental nudity to earthquakes.*

→ The proverb says that Providence protects children and idiots. This is really true. I know it because I have tested it.

→ We should be careful to get out of an experience only the wisdom that is in it— and stop there; lest we be like the cat that sits down on a hot stove-lid. She will never sit down on a hot stove-lid again—and that is well; but also she will never sit down on a cold one any more.

# Playing "Bear"

(from an autobiographical sketch, 1900)

This was in 1849. I was fourteen years old, then. We were still living in Hannibal, Missouri, on the banks of the Mississippi, in the new "frame" house built by my father five years before. That is, some of us lived in the new part, the rest in the old part back of it—the "L." In the autumn my sister gave a party, and invited all the marriageable young people of the village. I was too young for this society, and was too bashful to mingle with young ladies, anyway, therefore I was not invited—at least not for the whole evening. Ten minutes of it was to be my whole share. I was to do the part of a bear in a small fairy play. I was to be disguised all over in a close-fitting brown hairy stuff proper for a bear. About half past ten I was told to go to my room and put on this disguise, and be ready in half an hour. I started, but changed my mind; for I wanted to practise a little, and that room was very small. I crossed over to the large unoccupied house on the corner of Main and Hill streets,* unaware that a dozen of the young people were also going there to dress for their parts. I took the little black slave boy, Sandy, with me, and we selected a roomy and empty chamber on the second floor. We entered it talking, and this gave a couple of half-dressed young ladies an opportunity to take refuge behind a screen undiscovered. Their gowns and things were hanging on hooks behind the door, but I did not see them; it was Sandy that shut the door, but all his heart was in the theatricals, and he was as unlikely to notice them as I was myself.

That was a rickety screen, with many holes in it, but as I did not know there

---

*That house still stands.

were girls behind it, I was not disturbed by that detail. If I had known, I could not have undressed in the flood of cruel moonlight that was pouring in at the curtainless windows; I should have died of shame. Untroubled by apprehensions, I stripped to the skin and began my practice. I was full of ambition; I was determined to make a hit; I was burning to establish a reputation as a bear and get further engagements; so I threw myself into my work with an abandon that promised great things. I capered back and forth from one end of the room to the other on all fours, Sandy applauding with enthusiasm; I walked upright and growled and snapped and snarled; I stood on my head, I flung handsprings, I danced a lubberly dance with my paws bent and my imaginary snout sniffing from side to side; I did everything a bear could do, and many things which no bear could ever do and no bear with any dignity would want to do, anyway; and of course I never suspected that I was making a spectacle of myself to any one but Sandy. At last, standing on my head, I paused in that attitude to take a minute's rest. There was a moment's silence, then Sandy spoke up with excited interest and said—

"Marse Sam, has you ever seen a smoked herring?"

"No. What is that?"

"It's a fish."

"Well, what of it? Anything peculiar about it?"

"Yes, suh, you bet you dey is. *Dey eats 'em guts and all!*"

There was a smothered burst of feminine snickers from behind the screen! All the strength went out of me and I toppled forward like an undermined tower and brought the screen down with my weight, burying the young ladies under it. In their fright they discharged a couple of piercing screams—and possibly others, but I did not wait to count. I snatched my clothes and fled to the dark hall below, Sandy following. I was dressed in half a minute, and out the back way. I swore Sandy to eternal silence, then we went away and hid until the party was over. The ambition was all out of me. I could not have faced that giddy company after my adventure, for there would be two performers there who knew my secret, and would be privately laughing at me all the time. I was searched for but not found, and the bear had to be played by a young gentleman in his civilized clothes. The house was still and everybody asleep when I finally ventured home. I was very heavy-hearted, and full of a sense of disgrace. Pinned to my pillow I found a slip of paper which bore a line that did not lighten my heart, but only made my face burn. It was written in a laboriously disguised hand, and these were its mocking terms:

"You probably couldn't have played *bear,* but you played *bare* very well—oh, very very well!"

We think boys are rude, unsensitive animals, but it is not so in all cases. Each boy has one or two sensitive spots, and if you can find out where they are located you have only to touch them and you can scorch him as with fire. I suffered miserably over that episode. I expected that the facts would be all over the village in the morning, but it was not so. The secret remained confined to the two girls and Sandy and me. That was some appeasement of my pain, but it was far from sufficient—the main trouble remained: I was under four mocking eyes, and it might as well have been a thousand, for I suspected all girls' eyes of being the ones I so dreaded. During several weeks I could not look any young lady in the face; I dropped my eyes in confusion when any one of them smiled upon me and gave me greeting; and I said to myself, *"That is one of them,"* and got quickly away. Of course I was meeting the right girls everywhere, but if they ever let slip any betraying sign I was not bright enough to catch it. When I left Hannibal four years later, the secret was still a secret; I had never guessed those girls out, and was no longer expecting to do it. Nor wanting to, either.

One of the dearest and prettiest girls in the village at the time of my mishap was one whom I will call Mary Wilson, because that was not her name. She was twenty years old; she was dainty and sweet, peach-bloomy and exquisite, gracious and lovely in character, and I stood in awe of her, for she seemed to me to be made out of angel-clay and rightfully unapproachable by an unholy ordinary kind of a boy like me. I probably never suspected her. But—

The scene changes. To Calcutta—forty-seven years later. It was in 1896. I arrived there on my lecturing trip. As I entered the hotel a divine vision passed out of it, clothed in the glory of the Indian sunshine—the Mary Wilson of my long-vanished boyhood! It was a startling thing. Before I could recover from the bewildering shock and speak to her she was gone. I thought maybe I had seen an apparition, but it was not so, she was flesh. She was the grand-daughter of the other Mary, the original Mary. That Mary, now a widow, was up-stairs, and presently sent for me. She was old and gray-haired, but she looked young and was very handsome. We sat down and talked. We steeped our thirsty souls in the reviving wine of the past, the beautiful past, the dear and lamented past; we uttered the names that had been silent upon our lips for fifty years, and it was as if they were made of music; with reverent hands we unburied our dead, the mates of our youth, and caressed them with our speech; we searched the dusty chambers of our memories and dragged forth incident after incident, episode after episode, folly after folly, and laughed such good laughs over them, with the tears running down; and finally Mary said suddenly, and without any leading up—

"Tell me! What is the special peculiarity of smoked herrings?"

It seemed a strange question at such a hallowed time as this. And so inconsequential, too. I was a little shocked. And yet I was aware of a stir of some kind away back in the deeps of my memory somewhere. It set me to musing—thinking—searching. Smoked herrings. Smoked herrings. The peculiarity of smo . . . . I glanced up. Her face was grave, but there was a dim and shadowy twinkle in her eye which—All of a sudden I knew! and far away down in the hoary past I heard a remembered voice murmur, "Dey eats 'em guts and all!"

"At—last! I've found one of you, anyway! Who was the other girl?"

But she drew the line there. She wouldn't tell me.

#  An Apparition

(from *The Innocents Abroad*, 1869)

I remember yet how I ran off from school once, when I was a boy, and then, pretty late at night, concluded to climb into the window of my father's office and sleep on a lounge, because I had a delicacy about going home and getting thrashed. As I lay on the lounge and my eyes grew accustomed to the darkness, I fancied I could see a long, dusky, shapeless thing stretched upon the floor. A cold shiver went through me. I turned my face to the wall. That did not answer. I was afraid that that thing would creep over and seize me in the dark. I turned back and stared at it for minutes and minutes—they seemed hours. It appeared to me that the lagging moonlight never, never would get to it. I turned to the wall and counted twenty, to pass the feverish time away. I looked—the pale square was nearer. I turned again and counted fifty—it was almost touching it. With desperate will I turned again and counted one hundred, and faced about, all in a tremble. A white human hand lay in the moonlight! Such an awful sinking at the heart—such a sudden gasp for breath! I felt—I can not tell *what* I felt. When I recovered strength enough, I faced the wall again. But no boy could have remained so, with that mysterious hand behind him. I counted again, and looked—the most of a naked arm was exposed. I put my hands over my eyes and counted till I could stand it no longer, and then—the pallid face of a man was there, with the corners of the mouth drawn down, and the eyes fixed and glassy in death! I raised to a sitting posture and glowered on that corpse till the light crept down the bare breast,—line by line—inch by inch—past the nipple,—and then it disclosed a ghastly stab!

I went away from there. I do not say that I went away in any sort of a hurry, but I simply went—that is sufficient. I went out at the window, and I carried the sash along with me. I did not need the sash, but it was handier to take it than it was to leave it, and so I took it.

##  The Great Earthquake in San Francisco

(1865)

To-day's earthquake was no ordinary affair. It is likely that future earthquakes in this vicinity, for years to come, will suffer by comparison with it.

I have tried a good many of them here, and of several varieties—some that came in the form of a universal shiver; others that gave us two or three sudden upward heaves from below; others that swayed grandly and deliberately from side to side; and still others that came rolling and undulating beneath our feet like a great wave of the sea. But to-day's specimen belonged to a new, and, I hope, a very rare, breed of earthquakes. First, there was a quick, heavy shock; three or four seconds elapsed, and then the city and county of San Francisco darted violently from north-west to south-east, and from south-east to north-west five times with extraordinary energy and rapidity. I say "darted," because that word comes nearest to describing the movement.

I was walking along Third street, and facing north, when the first shock came; I was walking fast, and it "broke up my gait" pretty completely— checked me—just as a strong wind will do when you turn a corner and face it suddenly. That shock was coming from the north-west, and I met it halfway. I took about six or seven steps (went back and measured the distance afterwards to decide a bet about the interval of time between the first and second shocks), and was just turning the corner into Howard street when those five angry "darts" came. I suppose the first of them proceeded from the southeast, because it moved my feet toward the opposite point of the compass—to the left—and made me stagger against the corner house on my right. The noise accompanying the shocks was a tremendous rasping sound, like the violent shaking and grinding together of a block of brick houses. It was about the most disagreeable sound you can imagine.

I will set it down here as a maxim that the operations of the human intellect are much accelerated by an earthquake. Usually I do not think rapidly—but I did upon this occasion. I thought rapidly, vividly, and distinctly. With the first shock of the five, I thought—"I recognize that motion—this is an earthquake." With the second, I thought, "What a luxury this will be for the morning papers." With the third shock, I thought, "Well, my boy, you had better be getting out of this." Each of these thoughts was only the hundredth part of a second in passing through my mind. There is no incentive to rapid reasoning like an earthquake. I then sidled out toward the middle of the street—and I may say that I sidled out with some degree of activity, too. There is nothing like an earthquake to hurry a man up when he starts to go anywhere. As I went I glanced down to my left and saw the whole front of a large four-story brick building spew out and "splatter" abroad over the street in front of it. Another thought steamed through my brain. I thought this was going to be the greatest earthquake of the century, and that the city was going to be destroyed entirely, and I took out my watch and timed the event. It was twelve minutes to one o'clock, P.M. This showed great coolness and presence of mind on my part—most people would have been hunting for something to climb, instead of looking out for the best interests of history.

As I walked down the street—down the middle of the street—frequently glancing up with a sagacious eye at the houses on either side to see which way they were going to fall, I felt the earth shivering gently under me, and grew moderately sea-sick (and remained so for nearly an hour; others became ex-

"The 'one-horse shay' out-done." From the first American
edition of *Roughing It*, chapter 58.

cessively sleepy as well as sea-sick, and were obliged to go to bed, and refresh
themselves with a sound nap.) A minute before the earthquake I had three or
four streets pretty much to myself, as far as I could see down them (for we are
a Sunday-respecting community, and go out of town to break the Sabbath)
but five seconds after it I was lost in a swarm of crying children, and coatless,
hatless men and shrieking women. They were all in motion, too, and no two
of them trying to run in the same direction. They charged simultaneously from
opposite rows of houses, like opposing regiments from ambuscades, and came
together with a crash and a yell in the centre of the street. Then came chaos
and confusion, and a general digging out for somewhere else, they didn't know
where, and didn't care.

Everything that *was* done, was done in the twinkling of an eye—there was no apathy visible anywhere. A street car stopped close at hand, and disgorged its passengers so suddenly that they all seemed to flash out at the self-same instant of time.

The crowd was in danger from outside influences for a while. A horse was coming down Third street, with a buggy attached to him, and following after him—either by accident or design—and the horse was either frightened at the earthquake or a good deal surprised—I cannot say which, because I do not know how horses are usually affected by such things—but at any rate he must have been opposed to earthquakes, because he started to leave there, and took the buggy and his master with him, and scattered them over a piece of ground as large as an ordinary park, and finally fetched up against a lamp-post with nothing hanging to him but a few strips of harness suitable for fiddle-strings. However he might have been affected previously, the expression upon his countenance at this time was one of unqualified surprise. The driver of the buggy was found intact and unhurt, but to the last degree dusty and blasphemous. As the crowds along the street had fortunately taken chances on the earthquake and opened out to let the horse pass, no one was injured by his stampede.

When I got to the locality of the shipwrecked four-story building before spoken of, I found that the front of it, from eaves to pavement, had fallen out, and lay in ruins on the ground. The roof and floors were broken down and dilapidated. It was a new structure and unoccupied, and by rare good luck it damaged itself alone by its fall. The walls were only three bricks thick, a fact which, taking into account the earthquakiness of the country, evinces an unquestioning trust in Providence, on the part of the proprietor, which is as gratifying as it is impolitic and reckless.

I turned into Mission street and walked down to Second without finding any evidences of the great ague, but in Second street itself I traveled half a block on shattered window glass. The large hotels, farther down town, were all standing, but the boarders were all in the street. The plastering had fallen in many of the rooms, and a gentleman who was in an attic chamber of the Cosmopolitan at the time of the quake, told me the water "sloshed" out of the great tanks on the roof, and fell in sheets of spray to the court below. He said the huge building rocked like a cradle after the first grand spasms; the walls seemed to "belly" inward like a sail; and flakes of plastering began to drop on him. He then went out and slid, feet foremost down one or two hundred feet of banisters—partly for amusement, but chiefly with an eye to expedition. He said he flashed by the frantic crowds in each succeeding story like a telegraphic dispatch.

Several ladies felt a faintness and dizziness in the head, and one, (incredible as it may seem) weighing over two hundred and fifty pounds, fainted all over. They hauled her out of her room, and deluged her with water, but for nearly half an hour all efforts to resuscitate her were fruitless. It is said that the noise of the earthquake on the ground floor of the hotel, which is paved with marble, was as if forty freight trains were thundering over it. The large billiard saloon in the rear of the office was full of people at the time, but a moment afterward numbers of them were seen flying up the street with their billiard-cues in their hands, like a squad of routed lancers. Three jumped out of a back window into the central court, and found themselves imprisoned—for the tall, spike-armed iron gate which bars the passage-way for coal and provision wagons was locked.

"What did you do then?" I asked.

"Well, Conrad, from Humboldt—you know him—Conrad said, 'let's climb over, boys, and be devilish quick about it, too'—and he made a dash for it—but Smith and me started in last and were first over—because the seat of Conrad's pants caught on the spikes at the top, and we left him hanging there and yelling like an Injun."

And then my friend called my attention to the gate and said: "There's the gate—ten foot high, I should think, and nothing to catch hold of to climb by—but don't you know I went over that gate like a shot out of a shovel, and took my billiard-cue along with me?—I did it, as certain as I am standing here—but if I could do it again for fifteen hundred thousand dollars, I'll be d—d—not unless there was another earthquake, anyway."

From the fashionable barber-shops in the vicinity gentlemen rushed into the thronged streets in their shirt-sleeves, with towels round their necks, and with one side of their faces smoothly shaved, and the other side foamy with lather.

One gentleman was having his corns cut by a barber, when the premonitory shock came. The barber's under-jaw dropped, and he stared aghast at the dancing furniture. The gentleman winked complacently at the by-standers, and said with fine humor, "Oh, go on with your surgery, John—it's nothing but an earthquake; no use to run, you know, because if you're going to the devil anyhow, you might as well start from here as outside." Just then the earth commenced its hideous grinding and surging movement, and the gentleman retreated toward the door, remarking, "However, John, if we've *got* to go, perhaps we'd as well start from the street, after all."

On North Beach, men ran out of the bathing houses attired like the Greek slave, and mingled desperately with ladies and gentlemen who were as badly frightened as themselves, but more elaborately dressed.

The City Hall which is a large building, was so dismembered, and its walls sprung apart from each other, that the structure will doubtless have to be pulled down. The earthquake rang a merry peal on the City Hall bell, the "clapper" of which weighs seventy-eight pounds. It is said that several engine companies turned out, under the impression that the alarm was struck by the fire-telegraph.

Bells of all sorts and sizes were rung by the shake throughout the city, and from what I can learn the earthquake formally announced its visit on every door-bell in town. One gentleman said: "My door-bell fell to ringing violently, but I said to myself, 'I know *you*—you are an Earthquake; and you appear to be in a hurry; but you'll jingle that bell considerably before *I* let you in—on the contrary, I'll crawl under this sofa and get out of the way of the plastering.'"

I went down toward the city front and found a brick warehouse mashed in as if some foreigner from Brobdingnag had sat down on it.

All down Battery street the large brick wholesale houses were pretty universally shaken up, and some of them badly damaged, the roof of one being crushed in, and the fire-walls of one or two being ripped off even with the tops of the upper windows, and dumped into the street below.

The tall shot tower in First street weathered the storm, but persons who watched it respectfully from a distance said it swayed to and fro like a drunken giant.

I saw three chimneys which were broken in two about three feet from the top, and the upper sections slewed around until they sat corner-wise on the lower ones.

The damage done to houses by this earthquake is estimated at over half a million of dollars.

But I had rather talk about the "incidents." The Rev. Mr. Harmon, Principal of the Pacific Female Seminary, at Oakland, just across the Bay from here, had his entire flock of young ladies at church—and also his wife and children—and was watching and protecting them jealously, like one of those infernal scaly monsters with a pestilential breath that were employed to stand guard over imprisoned heroines in the days of chivalry, and who always proved inefficient in the hour of danger—he was watching them, I say, when the earthquake came, and what do you imagine he did, then? Why that confiding trust in Providence which had sustained him through a long ministerial career all at once deserted him, and he got up and ran like a quarter-horse. But that was not the misfortune of it. The exasperating feature of it was that his wife and children and all the school-girls remained bravely in their seats and sat the earthquake through without flinching. Oakland talks and laughs again at the Pacific Female Seminary.

The Superintendent of the Congregational Sunday School in Oakland had just given out the text, "And the earth shook and trembled," when the earthquake came along and took up the text and preached the sermon for him.

The Pastor of Starr King's church, the Rev. Mr. Stebbins, came down out of his pulpit after the first shock and embraced a woman. It was an instance of great presence of mind. Some say the woman was his wife, but I regard the remark as envious and malicious. Upon occasions like this, people who are too much scared to seize upon an offered advantage, are always ready to depreciate the superior judgment and sagacity of those who profited by the opportunity they lost themselves.

In a certain aristocratic locality up-town, the wife of a foreign dignitary is the acknowledged leader of fashion, and whenever she emerges from her house all the ladies in the vicinity fly to the windows to see what she has "got on," so that they may make immediate arrangements to procure similar costumes for themselves. Well, in the midst of the earthquake, the beautiful foreign woman (who had just indulged in a bath) appeared in the street *with a towel around her neck*. It was all the raiment she had on. Consequently, in that vicinity, a towel around the neck is considered the only orthodox "earthquake costume." Well, and why not? It is elegant, and airy, and simple, and graceful, and pretty, and are not these the chief requisites in female dress? If it were generally adopted it would go far toward reconciling some people to these dreaded earthquakes.

An enterprising barkeeper down town who is generally up with the times, has already invented a sensation drink to meet the requirements of our present peculiar circumstances. A friend in whom I have confidence, thus describes it to me: "A tall ale-glass is nearly filled with California brandy and Angelica wine—one part of the former to two of the latter; fill to the brim with champagne; charge the drink with electricity from a powerful galvanic battery, and swallow it before the lightning cools. Then march forth—and before you have gone a hundred yards you will think you are occupying the whole street; a parlor clock will look as big as a church; to blow your nose will astonish you like the explosion of a mine, and the most trivial abstract matter will seem as important as the Day of Judgment. When you want this extraordinary drink, disburse your twenty-five cents, and call for an 'EARTHQUAKE.'"

## Escape of the Tarantulas

(from *Roughing It*, 1872)

*Wishing to occupy his band of freeloading camp followers, the governor of Nevada Territory turns them into a surveying party. During their ineffectual daily labors the surveyors collect numerous tarantulas, which they keep in "covered tumblers" in their Carson City boarding house.*

The surveyors brought back more tarantulas with them, and so we had quite a menagerie arranged along the shelves of the room. Some of these spiders could straddle over a common saucer with their hairy, muscular legs, and when their feelings were hurt, or their dignity offended, they were the wickedest-looking desperadoes the animal world can furnish. If their glass prison-houses were touched ever so lightly they were up and spoiling for a fight in a minute. Starchy?—proud? Indeed, they would take up a straw and pick their teeth like a member of Congress. There was as usual a furious "zephyr" blowing the first night of the Brigade's return, and about midnight the roof of an adjoining stable blew off, and a corner of it came crashing through the side of our ranch. There was a simultaneous awakening, and a tumultuous muster of the Brigade in the dark, and a general tumbling and sprawling over each other in the narrow aisle between the bed-rows. In the midst of the turmoil, Bob H—— sprung up out of a sound sleep, and knocked down a shelf with his head. Instantly he shouted:

"Turn out, boys—the tarantulas is loose!"

No warning ever sounded so dreadful. Nobody tried, any longer, to leave the room, lest he might step on a tarantula. Every man groped for a trunk or a bed, and jumped on it. Then followed the strangest silence—a silence of grisly suspense it was, too—waiting, expectancy, fear. It was as dark as pitch, and one had to imagine the spectacle of those fourteen scant-clad men roosting gingerly on trunks and beds, for not a thing could be seen. Then came occasional little interruptions of the silence, and one could recognize a man and tell his locality by his voice, or locate any other sound a sufferer made by his gropings or changes of position. The occasional voices were not given to much speaking—you simply heard a gentle ejaculation of "Ow!" followed by a solid thump, and you knew the gentleman had felt a hairy blanket or something touch his bare skin and had skipped from a bed to the floor. Another silence. Presently you would hear a gasping voice say:

"Su-su-something's crawling up the back of my neck!"

Every now and then you could hear a little subdued scramble and a sorrowful "O Lord!" and then you knew that somebody was getting away from something he took for a tarantula, and not losing any time about it, either. Directly a voice in the corner rang out wild and clear:

"I've got him! I've got him!" [Pause, and probable change of circumstances.] "No, he's got me! Oh, ain't they *never* going to fetch a lantern!"

The lantern came at that moment, in the hands of Mrs. O'Flannigan, whose anxiety to know the amount of damage done by the assaulting roof had not prevented her waiting a judicious interval, after getting out of bed and lighting up, to see if the wind was done, now, up stairs, or had a larger contract.

The landscape presented when the lantern flashed into the room was picturesque, and might have been funny to some people, but was not to us. Although we were perched so strangely upon boxes, trunks and beds, and so strangely attired, too, we were too earnestly distressed and too genuinely miserable to see any fun about it, and there was not the semblance of a smile anywhere visible. I know I am not capable of suffering more than I did during those few minutes of suspense in the dark, surrounded by those creeping, bloody-minded tarantulas. I had skipped from bed to bed and from box to box in a cold agony, and every time I touched anything that was furzy I fancied I felt the fangs. I had rather go to war than live that episode over again. Nobody was hurt. The man who thought a tarantula had "got him" was mistaken—only a crack in a box had caught his finger. Not one of those escaped tarantulas was ever seen again. There were ten or twelve of them. We took candles and hunted the place high and low for them, but with no success. Did we go back to bed then? We did nothing of the kind. Money could not have persuaded us to do it. We sat up the rest of the night playing cribbage and keeping a sharp lookout for the enemy.

"The tarantula." From the first American edition of *Roughing It*, chapter 21.

# 🙟 Burglary and the Well-Tempered Householder 🙠

(from a 1906 autobiographical dictation)

*Among the items Mark Twain lost in this burglary, which seems to have occurred in February 1882, was his overcoat. As a result he hurried off coatless to an appointment in New York City and came under police scrutiny, as described in the next piece, "Under a Policeman's Eye."*

That burglar-alarm which Susy mentions led a gay and careless life, and had no principles. It was generally out of order at one point or another; and there was plenty of opportunity, because all the windows and doors in the house, from the cellar up to the top floor, were connected with it. However, in its seasons of being out of order it could trouble us for only a very little while: we quickly found out that it was fooling us, and that it was buzzing its blood-curdling alarm merely for its own amusement. Then we would shut it off, and send to New York for the electrician—there not being one in all Hartford in those days. When the repairs were finished we would set the alarm again and reestablish our confidence in it. It never did any real business except upon one single occasion. All the rest of its expensive career was frivolous and without purpose. Just that one time it performed its duty, and its whole duty—gravely, seriously, admirably. It let fly about two o'clock one black and dreary March morning, and I turned out promptly, because I knew that it was not fooling, this time. The bath-room door was on my side of the bed. I stepped in there, turned up the gas, looked at the annunciator, and turned off the alarm—so far as the door indicated was concerned—thus stopping the racket. Then I came back to bed.

Mrs. Clemens opened the debate:

"What was it?"

"It was the cellar door."

"Was it a burglar, do you think?"

"Yes," I said, "Of course it was. Do you suppose it was a Sunday-school superintendent?"

"No. What do you suppose he wants?"

"I suppose he wants jewelry, but he is not acquainted with the house and he thinks it is in the cellar. I don't like to disappoint a burglar whom I am not acquainted with, and who has done me no harm, but if he had had common sagacity enough to inquire, I could have told him we kept nothing down there but coal and vegetables. Still it may be that he *is* acquainted with the place, and that what he really wants is coal and vegetables. On the whole, I think it is vegetables he is after."

"Are you going down to see?"

"No; I could not be of any assistance. Let him select for himself; I don't know where the things are."

Then she said, "But suppose he comes up to the ground floor!"

"That's all right. We shall know it the minute he opens a door on that floor. It will set off the alarm."

Just then the terrific buzzing broke out again. I said,

"He has arrived. I told you he would. I know all about burglars and their ways. They are systematic people."

I went into the bath-room to see if I was right, and I was. I shut off the dining-room and stopped the buzzing, and came back to bed. My wife said,

"What do you suppose he is after now?"

I said, "I think he has got all the vegetables he wants and is coming up for napkin-rings and odds and ends for the wife and children. They all have families—burglars have—and they are always thoughtful of them, always take a few necessaries of life for themselves, and fill out with tokens of remembrance for the family. In taking them they do not forget us: those very things represent tokens of his remembrance of us, and also of our remembrance of him. We never get them again; the memory of the attention remains embalmed in our hearts."

"Are you going down to see what it is he wants now?"

"No," I said, "I am no more interested than I was before. They are experienced people,—burglars; *they* know what they want; I should be no help to him. I *think* he is after ceramics and bric-à-brac and such things. If he knows the house he knows that that is all that he can find on the dining-room floor."

She said, with a strong interest perceptible in her tone, "Suppose he comes up here!"

I said, "It is all right. He will give us notice."

"What shall we do then?"

"Climb out of the window."

She said, a little restively, "Well, what is the use of a burglar-alarm for us?"

"You have seen, dear heart, that it has been useful up to the present moment, and I have explained to you how it will be continuously useful after he gets up here."

That was the end of it. He didn't ring any more alarms.

Presently I said,

"He is disappointed, I think. He has gone off with the vegetables and the bric-à-brac, and I think he is dissatisfied."

We went to sleep, and at a quarter before eight in the morning I was out, and hurrying, for I was to take the 8.29 train for New York. I found the gas burning brightly—full head—all over the first floor. My new overcoat was gone; my old umbrella was gone; my new patent-leather shoes, which I had never worn, were gone. The large window which opened into the *ombra* at the rear of the house was standing wide. I passed out through it and tracked the burglar down the hill through the trees; tracked him without difficulty, because he had blazed his progress with imitation silver napkin-rings and my umbrella, and various other things which he had disapproved of; and I went back in triumph and proved to my wife that he *was* a disappointed burglar. I had suspected he would be, from the start, and from his not coming up to our floor to get human beings.

## Under a Policeman's Eye

(from "The Innocents Adrift," 1891–93)

*In rural France in August 1891, while staying at the rustic, family-run Hôtel du Rhône Moine, which catered to "foot wanderers and laborers," Clemens recalled an uneasy encounter with a New York policeman that had taken place almost a decade earlier.*

We went to bed early. It is inside the house, not outside, that one really finds the peasant life. Our rooms were over the stable, and this was not an advantage. The cows and horses were not very quiet, the smell was extraordinary, the fleas were a disorderly lot, and these things helped the coffee to keep us awake. We slept none, but visited back and forth all night. The family went to bed at 9 and got up at 2. The beds were very high; one could not climb into them without the help of a chair; and as they were narrow and arched, there was danger of rolling out in case one drifted into dreams of an imprudent sort. These lofty bedsteads were not high from caprice, but for a purpose—they contained chests of drawers, and the drawers were full of clothing and other family property. On the table in my room were some bright-colored—even gorgeous—little waxen saints and a Virgin under bell-glasses; also the treasures of the house—jewelry and a silver watch. It was not costly jewelry, but it was jewelry, at any rate, and without doubt the family valued it. I judged that this household were accustomed to having honest guests and neighbors or they would have removed these things from the room when I entered it, for I do not look honester than others.

Not that I have always thought in this way about myself, for I haven't. I thought the reverse until the time I lost my overcoat, once, when I was going down to New York to see the Water Color exhibition, and had a sort of adventure in consequence. The house had been robbed in the night, and when I came down stairs to rush for the early train there was no overcoat. It was a raw day, and when I got to New York at noon I grew colder and colder as I walked along down the avenue. When I reached East 34th street I stopped on the corner and began to consider. It seemed to me that it must have been just about there that Smith,* the artist, took me one winter's night, with others, five years before, and caroused us with roasted oysters and Southern stories and hilarity in his fourth story until three or four in the morning; and now if I could only call to mind which of those houses over the way was his, I could borrow an overcoat. All the time that I was standing there thinking and trying to recollect, I was dimly conscious of a figure near me, but only dimly, very dimly; but now as I came out of my reverie and found myself gazing, rapt but totally unconscious, at one of the houses over there, that figure solidified itself and became at once the most conspicuous thing in the landscape. It was a policeman. He was standing not six feet away, and was gazing as intently at my face as I had been gazing at the house. I was embarrassed—it is always embarrassing to come to yourself and find a stranger staring at you. You blush, even when you have not been doing any harm. So I blushed—a

*Note, 1904. Hopkinson Smith, now a distinguished man, in literature, art, and architecture. SLC.

thing which does not commend a person to a policeman; also I tried to smile a placating smile, but it did not get any response, so then I tried to make it a kind of friendly smile, which was a mistake, because that only hardens a policeman, and I saw at once that this smile had hardened this one and made my situation more difficult than ever; and so, naturally, my judgment being greatly impaired by now, I spoke—which was an error, because in these circumstances one cannot arrange without reflection a remark which will not seem to have a kind of suspicious something about it to a policeman, and that was what happened this time; for I fanned-up that haggard smile again, which had been dying out when I wasn't noticing, and said—

"Could you tell me, please, if there's a Mr. Smith lives over there in—"

"*What* Smith?"

That rude abruptness drove his other name out of my mind; and as I saw I never should be able to think of it with the policeman standing there cowing me with his eye, that way, it seemed to me best to get out a name of some kind, so as to avert further suspicion, therefore I brought out the first one which came into my mind, which was John—another error. The policeman turned purple—apparently with a sense of injury and insult; and said there were a million John Smiths in New York, and *which* one was this? Also, what did I want with Smith? I could not remember—the overcoat was gone out of my mind. So I told him he was a pupil of mine and that I was giving him lessons in morals; moral culture—a new system.

That was a lucky hit, anyway. I was merely despicable, now, to the policeman, but harmless—I could see it in his eye. He looked me over, a moment, then said—

"You give him lessons, do you?"

"Yes, sir."

"How long have you been giving him lessons?"

"Two years, next month." I was getting my wind again—and confidence.

"Which house does he live in?"

"That one—the middle one in the block."

"Then what did you ask *me* for, a minute ago?"

I did not see my way out. He waited for an answer, but got tired before I could think of one that would fit the case, and said—

"How is it that you haven't an overcoat on, such a day as this?"

"I—well, I never wear them. It doesn't seem cold to me."

He thought awhile, with his eye on me, then said, with a sort of sigh—

"Well, maybe you are all right—I don't know—but you want to walk pretty straight while you're on *my* beat; for, morals or no morals, blamed if I take much stock in you. Move on, now."

Then he turned away, swinging his club by its string. But his eye was over his shoulder, my way; so I had to cross to that house, though I didn't want to, any more. I did not expect it to be Smith's house, now that I was so out of luck, but I thought I would ring and ask, and if it proved to be some one else's house then I would explain that I had come to examine the gas meter, and thus get out the back way and be all right again. The door was opened by a middle-aged matron with a gentle and friendly face, and she had a sweet serenity about her that was a notable contrast to my nervous flurry. I asked after Smith, and if he lived there, and to my surprise and gratitude she said that this was his home.

"Can I see him? Can I see him right away?—immediately!"

No, he was gone down town. My rising hopes fell to ruin.

"Then can I see Mrs. Smith?"

But alas and alas, she was gone down town with him. In my distress I was suddenly smitten by one of those ghastly hysterical inspirations, you know, when you want to do an insane thing just to astonish and petrify somebody; so I said with a rather overdone pretence of playful ease and assurance—

"Ah, this is a very handsome overcoat on the hat-rack—be so good as to lend it to me for a day or two!"

"With pleasure," she said—and she had the coat on me before I knew what had happened. It had been my idea to astonish and petrify her, but I was the person astonished and petrified, myself. So astonished and so petrified, in fact, that I was out of the house and gone, without a thank-you or a question, before I came to my senses again. Then I drifted slowly along, reflecting—reflecting pleasantly. I said to myself, "She simply divined my character by my face—what a far clearer intuition she has than that policeman." The thought sent a glow of self-satisfaction through me.

Then a hand was laid on my shoulder and I shrunk together with a crash. It was the policeman. He scanned me austerely, and said—

"Where did you get that overcoat?"

Although I had not been doing any harm I had all the sense of being caught—caught in something disreputable. The officer's accusing eye and unbelieving aspect heightened this effect. I told what had befallen me at the house in as straightforward a way as I could, but I was ashamed of the tale, and looked it, without doubt, for I knew and felt how improbable it must necessarily sound to anybody, particularly a policeman. Manifestly he did not believe me. He made me tell it all over again, then he questioned me:

"You don't know the woman?"

"No, I don't know her."

"Haven't the least idea who she is?"

"Not the least."

"You didn't tell her your name?"

"No."

"She didn't ask for it?"

"No."

"You just asked her to lend you the overcoat, and she let you take it?"

"She put it on me herself."

"And didn't look frightened?"

"Frightened?—of course not."

"Nor even surprised?"

"Not in the slightest degree."

He paused. Presently he said—

"My friend, I don't believe a word of it. Don't you see, yourself, it's a tale that won't wash? Do *you* believe it?"

"Yes. I know it's true."

"Warn't you surprised?"

"Clear through to the marrow!"

He had been edging me along back toward the house. He had a deep design; he sprung it on me, now; said he—

"Stop where you are—I'll mighty soon find out!"

He walked to the door and up the steps, keeping a furtive eye out toward me and ready to jump for me if I ran. Then he pretended to pull the bell, and instantly faced about to observe the effect on me. But there wasn't any; I walked toward him instead of running away. That unsettled him. He came down the steps, evidently perplexed, and said—

"Well, *I* can't make it out. It may be all right, but it's too many for me. I don't like your looks and I won't have such characters around. Go along, now, and look sharp; if I catch you prowling around here again, I'll run you *in*."

I found Smith at the Water Color dinner that night, and asked him if it was merely my face that had enabled me to borrow the overcoat from a stranger, but he was surprised, and said—

"*No!* What an idea—and what intolerable conceit! She is my housekeeper, and remembered your drawling voice from overhearing it a moment that night four or five years ago in my house; so she knew where to send the police if you didn't bring the coat back."

After all those years I was sitting here, now, at midnight in the peasant hotel, in my night clothes, and honoring womankind in my thoughts; for here was another woman, with the noble and delicate intuitions of her sex, trusting me, a total stranger, with all her modest wealth. She entered the room, just then, and stood beaming upon me a moment with her sweet matronly eyes, then took away the jewelry.

# ✦ About the Texts ✦

The following notes briefly identify persons, places, and events mentioned in the texts, record the sources of the quoted maxims, and provide background information about the images that introduce the eight chapters. Unless otherwise noted here or in the illustration captions, all the images in this volume are reproduced from originals in the Mark Twain Papers collection.

Most of the fifty-one pieces in this collection come from published sources, often newspapers, periodicals, or first editions of longer works published during Mark Twain's lifetime. The remaining texts come from manuscript or, in the case of Mark Twain's autobiographical dictations, typescript. The notes indicate whether the text is complete or an excerpt from a longer work. Where possible, the texts are drawn from the Mark Twain Project's University of California Press editions.

Thirty-eight of the texts have nonauthorial descriptive titles supplied by the editors of this volume. The remaining thirteen titles were Mark Twain's own or were supplied by the original publishers: "Be Good, Be Good. *A Poem*"; "Breaking It Gently"; "At the Funeral"; "A Telephonic Conversation"; "An Appeal against Injudicious Swearing"; "Political Economy"; "Notice. To the Next Burglar"; "The 'Wake-Up-Jake'"; "Experience of the McWilliamses with Membranous Croup"; "The Late Benjamin Franklin"; "Advice to Youth"; "A Fashion Item"; and "The Great Earthquake in San Francisco."

There has been very little editorial intervention in the texts, but in a few cases such intervention was needed. In the manuscript for "At the Funeral," for instance, where Mark Twain supplied a possible alternative to his original reading but left both standing, the later reading is adopted ("suffers no inconvenience" replaces "derives no suffering"). In the published version of Mark Twain's seventieth-birthday speech that supplies the text for "Smoking, Diet, and Health at Age Seventy," a reading crucial to sense was inadvertently omitted. It has been supplied from four contemporary newspaper transcriptions of the same speech ("if I should break it I should" replaces "I would"). Although the first printing of "The Late Benjamin Franklin" is the source of the present text, Mark Twain's small correction for a later printing is adopted here ("desire" for "desired"). In addition, a few necessary editorial corrections have been made to the texts throughout, to supply missing punctuation or correct typographical errors. For instance, in the manuscript that supplies the text for "A Sampling of Childish Ethics," Mark Twain has an opening but not a closing square bracket. The missing bracket is editorially supplied. In "Breaking It Gently," the editors supply "Bagley" for the *Galaxy*'s mistaken "Bgaley" and, in "The Hand of Fashion," "soliloquized" for "solilopuized," the reading of the first edition of *The Innocents Abroad*.

In the texts, all ampersands are rendered as "and" except in private letters, where they are preserved. All full-size square brackets are Mark Twain's. Editorial brackets supplying necessary corrections are all either subscript or superscript. All ellipses in the texts are editorial except for the following three instances, which are Mark Twain's: "About American Manners" ("Well . . . . no"); "Experience of the McWilliamses with Membranous Croup" ("frantic! . . . . . There"); and "Playing 'Bear'" ("smo . . . . I"). Certain minor stylistic features of the original printings are not followed here. For instance, the variously styled salutations and signatures in letters drawn from newspapers have been rendered capital and lowercase.

FRONTISPIECE: When Stormfield was burglarized at 12:30 A.M. on 18 September 1908, it was Mark Twain's secretary, Isabel V. Lyon, who sounded the alarm and woke the household; the butler fired at the fleeing burglars. Shaken by the event, the servants resigned in its aftermath, and Clara Clemens sought refuge in New York. Mark Twain, on the other hand, followed the capture and trial of the burglars with interest. He posed with a gun for Lyon, an amateur photographer, "showing how he would attack the burglars," as Lyon noted in her album.

BOOK EPIGRAPH: "The human race consists" and "Good friends, good books, and a sleepy conscience" are from the notebook Mark Twain kept between 1897 and 1900, Notebook 42 at the Mark Twain Papers, The Bancroft Library.

## I. EVERYDAY ETIQUETTE

Illustration (page 12): This is the first in a series of seven photographs of Mark Twain taken by his biographer, Albert Bigelow Paine, in the summer of 1906, while the author was vacationing in Dublin, New Hampshire. Mark Twain numbered and captioned the photographs and then inserted them into the typescript of his autobiographical dictation of 31 August 1906, explaining,

> I wish to insert a set of them here for future generations to study, with the result, I hope, that they will reform, if they need it—and I expect they will. I am sending half a dozen of these sets to friends of mine who need reforming, and I have introduced the pictures to them with this formula: This series of photographs registers with scientific precision, stage by stage, the progress of a moral purpose through the mind of the human race's Oldest Friend.

The final photograph in the series is reproduced on page 33.

Maxims (page 14): "The highest perfection of politeness" is from "On the Decay of the Art of Lying" in *The Stolen White Elephant, Etc.* (220–21). "Etiquette requires us" is from the notebook Mark Twain kept in 1902: Notebook 45 at the Mark Twain Papers, The Bancroft Library.

A Letter of Apology (page 15): Mark Twain's letter of 14 June 1876 to "Miss Harriet" (not further identified), from which this text is excerpted, is at the Clifton Waller Barrett Library, University of Virginia.

About the Effect of Intemperate Language (pages 15–19): This excerpt is taken from the autobiographical dictation of 9 February 1906 at the Mark Twain Papers, The Bancroft Library, as revised by Mark Twain and published in the 2 November 1906 *North American Review* (183:833–36). Clemens and Olivia L. Langdon had married on 2 February 1870, so the incident he describes here probably occurred around 1880.

Be Good, Be Good. *A Poem.* (pages 19–20): This text is taken from the manuscript poem of 14 November 1908 to Margaret Blackmer of New York, at the Clifton Waller Barrett Library, University of Virginia.

An Innovative Dinner Party Signal System (pages 20–22): This excerpt is taken from the autobiographical dictation of 5 March 1906 at the Mark Twain Papers, The Bancroft Library. The dictation was first published in the 1924 *Mark Twain's Autobiography* (1:156–58). In the last paragraph Clemens alludes to his account, in chapter 47 of *Roughing It* (1872), of how Buck Fanshaw put down an election riot "before it got a start."

About American Manners (page 23): This excerpt is taken from an untitled manuscript draft of a speech at the Mark Twain Papers, The Bancroft Library. This speech, perhaps delivered in early 1906, introduced Henry Van Dyke, noted clergyman and professor of English literature at Princeton. Albert Bigelow Paine titled it "Introducing Doctor Van Dyke" when he published it in 1923 in *Mark Twain's Speeches* (296–301).

Breaking It Gently (page 24): This anecdote first appeared as an untitled item in Mark Twain's monthly "Memoranda" column in the *Galaxy* magazine of June 1870 (9:862). It appeared under the present title in 1872 in *Mark Twain's Sketches* (London: George Routledge and Sons), a collection "selected and revised" by the author.

Courtesy to Unexpected Visitors (pages 25–26): No manuscript survives for Mark Twain's speech of 7 March 1906 at Barnard College in New York City. This excerpt is reprinted from the 1910 edition of *Mark Twain's Speeches* (235–37). Sylvester was modeled after the Clemens family's butler, George Griffin (1849?–97), a former slave who came one day in 1875 to wash some windows and remained until 1891. In 1906 Clemens described him as "handsome, well built, shrewd, wise, polite, always good-natured, cheerful to gaiety, honest, religious, a cautious truth-speaker, devoted friend to the family, champion of its interests, a sort of idol to the children" ("A Family Sketch"). Onteora Park, in the Catskill Mountains, was the site of an artists' and literary colony that the Clemenses had visited briefly in August 1885 and from July through September 1890. The unfortunate visitor, who had met Olivia Clemens there in 1890, was Benjamin E. Martin, a Civil War surgeon and later an author of travel books. Olivia had instructed Griffin to tell Clemens to entertain Martin, contravening Clemens's prior order that Griffin not disturb him for any reason. The Wintons are fictitious stand-ins for the Clemenses' neighbors Charles Dudley Warner and Susan Lee Warner.

At the Funeral (page 27): This piece is from an unfinished manuscript, an attempt at a burlesque of etiquette manuals that Mark Twain worked on in 1881, at the Mark Twain Papers, The Bancroft Library. Paine published some sections of the manuscript in *Mark Twain: A Biography* (2:705–6).

A Telephonic Conversation (pages 28–32): The text of this piece is from its first publication in the *Atlantic Monthly* of June 1880 (45:841–43). The telephone was perfected by Alexander Graham Bell in March 1876, and the Bell Telephone Company was organized in July 1877. Within six months Clemens had a telephone in his home and was part of a limited Hartford network. By 1879, a year before Clemens published the present sketch, the Hartford telephone network had expanded, and he was listed in the local directory. Although a William I. Bagley, a printer, lived in Hartford in 1880, the family of that name mentioned here probably was fictitious.

## 2. MODEST PROPOSALS AND JUDICIOUS COMPLAINTS

Illustration (page 34): This hand-lettered and hand-colored "Notice"—probably the one posted on the front door of the house, as reported in Mark Twain's autobiographical dictation of 6 October 1908—was the work of a young visitor, one of Mark Twain's "angelfish," sixteen-year-old Dorothy Sturgis, whose name appears in the cartouche at the lower left. Sturgis arrived at Stormfield for a visit on the evening of 18 September 1908, just a few hours after the Stormfield burglary.

Maxims (page 36): "Nothing so needs reforming" is from "Pudd'nhead Wilson's Calendar" in *Pudd'nhead Wilson*, chapter 15. "When I reflect" is from "Pudd'nhead Wilson's Calendar" in *Pudd'nhead Wilson*, chapter 13.

A Christmas Wish (page 37): Mark Twain's letter of 23 December 1890 to the editor of the *New York World* was published under the title "Christmas Greetings" in the *World* of 25 December (1), from which this text is taken. The *World* had solicited "a handful of Christmas sentiments from women and men who have earned the right to be listened to when they speak." The other contributors were authors Joel Chandler Harris, Oliver Wendell Holmes, Elizabeth Stuart Phelps, James Whitcomb Riley, Frank Stockton, and Ella Wheeler Wilcox; author and orator George William Curtis; author, journalist, and lecturer Kate Field; and clergymen John Philip Newman and David Swing. The editor of the *World* was Joseph Pulitzer. In 1925, in a memoir written for her (Mary Lawton, *A Lifetime with Mark Twain*), Katy Leary, Clemens's longtime maid, recalled that Alexander Graham Bell wrote to Clemens, appealing his exclusion from Clemens's benediction. Clemens later extended his blessing to Bell.

Proposal Regarding Local Flooding (pages 38–41): Mark Twain's letter of 30 March 1873 to the editor of the *Hartford Courant* was published in the *Courant* of 31 March under the title "A Horrible Tale. Fearful Calamity in Forest Street" (2). It was reprinted in *Mark Twain's Letters, Volume 5* (325–28), from which this text is taken. In this humorous protest about the condition of Hartford's Forest Street, Clemens was speaking from close personal experience. He and his family lived in a rented house there from 1871 until 1874. The editors of the *Hartford Courant* were Clemens's friends Joseph R. Hawley and Charles Dudley Warner. Warner was in charge of the paper whenever Hawley, editor in chief, was in Washington at his post as a Republican congressman. Except for Hartford attorney Franklin Chamberlin and Warner's brother George, mentioned in the first and second paragraphs, respectively, the characters in Clemens's mock drama are fictitious. "Probabilities," mentioned at the end of the letter, was a standard part of the *Courant*'s daily weather column.

Complaint about Unreliable Service (pages 41–42): The text of Mark Twain's letter of 12 February 1891 to the Hartford City Gas Light Company is that of the manuscript in the Mark Twain Papers, The Bancroft Library. The danger Clemens complained of was real. Since the gas fixtures in his house had to be manually lit, a shutdown of the gas service followed by an unannounced start-up posed a genuine threat of asphyxiation and conflagration.

Notice about a Stolen Umbrella (page 42): Mark Twain's letter of 18 or 19 May 1875 to the public was published in the *Hartford Courant* of 20 May in "New Advertisements" (3) and reprinted in *Mark Twain's Letters, Volume 6* (481), from which this text is taken. This comic notice drew comment, in Hartford and elsewhere, for months. Some of it was unappreciative. The *New York World*, for example, took Mark Twain to task for potentially inciting murder. Subsequently, a mischievous report circulated in the press, and was taken seriously by some, that a boy's body had been left on his doorstep.

An Appeal against Injudicious Swearing (pages 43–44): This letter to the editor was first published in the *New York Sun* of 9 November 1890 (6), from which this text is taken. The *Sun*'s editor, Charles A. Dana, and its publisher, William M. Laffan, were good friends of Clemens's.

An Unwanted Magazine Subscription (page 45): The text of Mark Twain's letter of 18 February 1883 to J. W. Bouton of New York City is that of the manuscript in the Mark Twain Papers, The Bancroft Library. James W. Bouton was a New York rare-book dealer and publisher. He may have been an agent for *The Portfolio: An Artistic Periodical*, published in London. In March 1883 Clemens gave in and paid Bouton's bill. Daniel Slote and Company was a New York blank book and stationery firm in which Clemens's friend Daniel Slote had been a partner until his death in 1882.

On Telephones and Swearing (pages 46–47): This excerpt is taken from the autobiographical dictation of 30 August 1906 at the Mark Twain Papers, The Bancroft Library. Clemens's "New York home" was a rented house at 21 Fifth Avenue, on the corner of Ninth Street, which he shared with his daughters, Clara and Jean, and his secretary, Isabel V. Lyon. The "nameless manuscript" (with the distinctive opening remark) that he wished Clara to retrieve was a story he began in March 1905 and later referred to as "The Refuge of the Derelicts" but never completed. It is published in *Mark Twain's Fables of Man* (162–248). Mr. Scovel remains unidentified.

About the Proposed Street-Widening (page 48): This excerpt from Mark Twain's letter of 8 May 1874 to Charles E. Perkins of Hartford, Connecticut, is taken from the manuscript at the Mark Twain House, Hartford, as published in *Mark Twain's Letters, Volume 6* (139). Clemens sent this letter from Quarry Farm, his sister-in-law Susan Crane's home on East Hill in Elmira, New York, where he and his family spent summers in order to escape the Hartford heat. He wrote much of his best work at Quarry Farm—including *Tom Sawyer* (1876) and a large part of *Huckleberry Finn* (1885)—in the airy octagonal study that Crane built for him. Charles E. Perkins was Clemens's Hartford friend, neighbor, and lawyer. Ezra Hall, another neighbor, also was a prominent Hartford attorney.

Political Economy (pages 49–56): This sketch first appeared in Mark Twain's monthly "Memoranda" column in the *Galaxy* magazine of September 1870 (10:424–26). It is reprinted here from the *Galaxy*. Nineteenth-century political economy was a social science concerned with governmental, rather than commercial or personal, economics. Clemens alludes in passing to Persian religious teacher and prophet Zoroaster (ca. 628–551 B.C.); Horace Greeley (1811–72), reformist founder, publisher, and editor of the *New York Tribune;* the Colossus of Rhodes, one of the seven wonders of the ancient world, a large bronze statue of the sun god, Helios, erected in the harbor of Rhodes between 292 and 280 B.C.; phlogiston ("dephlogistic"), a hypothetical substance believed by early chemists to be essential to combustion; the Chinese sage Confucius (ca. 551–479 B.C.); Roman orator, statesman, and philosopher Marcus Tullius Cicero (106–43 B.C.); English poet George Gordon Byron (1788–1824); Greek poet Homer (dates uncertain); and Jewish historian and soldier Flavius Josephus (37–?95).

Notice. To the Next Burglar (pages 56–57): This excerpt is taken from the autobiographical dictation of 6 October 1908 at the Mark Twain Papers, The Bancroft Library.

Suggestion to Persons Entering Heaven (page 57): This excerpt is from an untitled manuscript written by Clemens in Bermuda in late March 1910, at Washington University in St. Louis, Missouri. Albert Bigelow Paine later titled it "Advice to Paine" and published extracts from it in *Mark Twain: A Biography* (3:1566–67).

## 3. THE AMERICAN TABLE

Illustration (page 58): On 11 January 1908, Mark Twain was honored for the third time with a dinner at New York City's Lotos Club, whose membership was largely drawn from literary, theatrical, and artistic circles. Mark Twain had been elected to the club in 1873 and delivered dinner speeches there on several occasions, including the present one. The fare included "Innocent Oysters Abroad," "Gilded Age Duck," and "Prince and the Pauper Cakes."

Maxims (page 60): "The true Southern watermelon" is from "Pudd'nhead Wilson's Calendar" in *Pudd'nhead Wilson*, chapter 14. "The widow rung a bell for supper" is from *Adventures of Huckleberry Finn*, chapter 1.

Memories of Food on an American Farm (pages 61–62): This excerpt is taken from Mark Twain's 1897–98 manuscript "My Autobiography [Random Extracts from it.]," at the Mark Twain Papers, The Bancroft Library. A version of the text was first published in the 1 March 1907 *North American Review* (184:452–53).

American versus European Food (pages 63–68): This extract from chapter 49 of *A Tramp Abroad* is taken from the American Publishing Company's 1880 first edition (571–75). Clemens's "sincere and capable refrigerator" was an icebox. Although mechanical vapor-compression refrigerators, employing ammonia, sulfur dioxide, methyl ether, and methyl chloride as coolants, were in commercial use by the 1870s, their cost, size, and complexity, and the toxicity and flammability of the coolants, prevented any widespread home use.

An Inauspicious Meal (pages 68–71): This extract from chapter 4 of *Roughing It* is reprinted from the Mark Twain Project's 1993 edition (21–26). Queensware was cream-colored pottery first manufactured in the 1760s by Josiah Wedgwood for Queen Charlotte of England and named in her honor. Nicolson pavement, patented by Samuel Nicolson in 1854, was popular in American cities of the 1860s. It was made up of a bed of sand upon which were laid inch-thick boards, a coat of asphalt, wooden blocks fixed in place with board strips and coal and pebbles, hot tar to fill all chinks, and a final covering of coarse sand or pebbles.

A Remarkable Dinner (pages 72–78): This extract from chapter 11 of *The Gilded Age* is reprinted from the American Publishing Company's 1873 first edition (108–13). "Roderick Dhu" was a character in Sir Walter Scott's poem "The Lady of the Lake." "Baron Poniatowski" possibly was Prince Józef Michał Poniatowski (1816–73), a Polish composer who resided in Paris and was made a senator by Napoleon III. "Old Dr. McDowells" was Joseph Nash McDowell (1805–68), a brilliant and eccentric surgeon who in 1840 helped found Missouri Medical College, the first medical school in St. Louis. Colonel Sellers's "eye-water," first introduced in chapter 8, was his "Infallible Imperial Oriental Optic Liniment and Salvation for Sore Eyes," which was "a kind of decoction nine-tenths water and the other tenth drugs that don't cost more than a dollar a barrel." He had not managed "to hit upon" the "one ingredient wanted yet to perfect the thing." Once he found it, he planned to flood the world with the product and reap millions in profits. In early copies of *The Gilded Age,* the colonel's first name was "Eschol," but when a real George Escol Sellers threatened a lawsuit, the name was changed to "Beriah."

Food and Scenery (pages 78–79): This extract from chapter 17 of *Roughing It* is reprinted from the Mark Twain Project's 1993 edition (120–21).

## 4. TRAVEL MANNERS

Illustration (page 80): Frontispiece from the first American edition of *Following the Equator.* The image of Mark Twain relaxing aboard the steamer *Warrimoo,* en route from Vancouver to Australia, was taken in 1895 by a fellow passenger.

Maxims (page 82): "Travel is fatal to prejudice, bigotry and narrow-mindedness" is from *The Innocents Abroad,* conclusion. "The gentle reader" is from *The Innocents Abroad,* chapter 23.

Traveling in Close Quarters (pages 83–85): This extract from chapter 2 of *Roughing It* is reprinted from the Mark Twain Project's 1993 edition (7–9). In remarking of the loquacious passenger that "the fountains of her great deep were broken up," Clemens alluded to one of his favorite biblical passages, Genesis 7:11: "The same day were all the fountains of the great deep broken up, and the windows of heaven were opened."

Communicating with the Locals (pages 85–87): This extract from chapter 19 of *The Innocents Abroad* is reprinted from the American Publishing Company's 1869 first edition (187–89). This episode includes characters based on two of Mark Twain's closest friends during the steamer *Quaker City*'s excursion to Europe and the Holy Land: Daniel Slote (1828?–82), his cabin mate, a New York stationer; and Dr.

Abraham Reeves Jackson (1827–92), of Stroudsburg, Pennsylvania, a Civil War veteran who became a prominent gynecologist. Blucher was based on another passenger who sometimes joined Clemens's party, Frederick H. Greer, of Boston.

A Night Excursion in a Hotel Room (pages 87–93): This extract from chapter 13 of *A Tramp Abroad* is taken from the American Publishing Company's 1880 first edition (114–21). The prototype for Harris was Clemens's good friend Joseph H. Twichell, pastor of Hartford's Asylum Hill Congregational Church. Twichell was Clemens's travel companion for part of the extended European excursion described in *A Tramp Abroad*.

## 5. HEALTH AND DIET

Illustration (page 94): The article "Mark Twain: Pioneer on Fasting and Health" by George Wharton James, in the May 1919 issue of *Physical Culture* magazine, argued for the restorative effects of a near-starvation diet and cited Mark Twain's essays "My Début as a Literary Person" (1899) and "At the Appetite-Cure" (1898) as evidence of the author's interest in this subject. James's article was illustrated by five previously unpublished photographs of Mark Twain, including the cover photograph, taken by the New York City photographer A. Frederick Bradley at his Fifth Avenue studio in the spring of 1907. Bradley positioned his subject on a revolving stand and took seventeen photos at the sitting. Four of them Clemens reportedly called "the finest photographs of himself that had ever been taken." Note for the curious regarding the article by George Bernard Shaw advertised on the cover of *Physical Culture:* Shaw stated unequivocally that child beating was "a form of debauchery" and that to treat a child "as a pet animal to be trained by the whip simply to give no trouble to its elders, results—well, in the sort of people we have at present, trying to conduct whole civilizations as if they were dog kennels."

Maxims (page 96): "He had had much experience of physicians" is from "Pudd'nhead Wilson's New Calendar" in *Following the Equator,* chapter 49. "As an example to others" is from Mark Twain's speech at the dinner celebrating his seventieth birthday, 5 December 1905, as published in the 1910 edition of *Mark Twain's Speeches* (258).

Young Sam Clemens and Old-Time Doctoring (pages 97–99): This excerpt is taken from Mark Twain's 1897–98 manuscript "My Autobiography [Random Extracts from it.]," at the Mark Twain Papers, The Bancroft Library, as revised by Mark Twain and published in the 1 March 1907 *North American Review* (184:457–59). Clemens was born in the village of Florida, in northeastern Missouri, on 30 November 1835. His family moved to nearby Hannibal in 1839. He was treated in both villages by Dr. Hugh Meredith (1806–64) and may have been treated by Dr. Thomas J. Chowning as well. Mrs. Utterback has not been precisely identified, although there were Utterbacks in Missouri. Clemens liked the name and used it in his fiction, for example, "old Mother Utterback" in an 1866 sketch, "Captain Montgomery," and "sister Utterback" in chapter 41 of *Huckleberry Finn* (1885).

The "Wake-Up-Jake" (pages 99–101): The text of this extract from Mark Twain's 23 August 1863 letter to the *Virginia City Territorial Enterprise* is taken from the Mark Twain Project's 1979 *Early Tales & Sketches, Volume 1* (275–76). Clemens sampled the explosive purgative known as the "wake-up-Jake" in Steamboat Springs, Nevada Territory, at the hospital and baths operated by Dr. Joseph Ellis. The friends he mentions were W. A. Palmer, a Wells Fargo agent in Folsom, California; Adair Wilson, local editor of the *Virginia City Union;* and Clement T. Rice ("the Unreliable"), a respected *Union* reporter with whom Clemens, on the staff of the rival *Territorial Enterprise*, had a mock journalistic feud. The "servants of the lamp" were genies.

A Healthful Cocktail (pages 101–2): The text of Samuel Clemens's letter of 2 January 1874 to Olivia Clemens is taken from the manuscript in the Mark Twain Papers, The Bancroft Library, as published in *Mark Twain's Letters, Volume 6* (3). When he wrote this letter, Clemens was finishing a highly successful English lecture engagement and had not seen his wife, who was awaiting him at home in Hartford, Connecticut, for nearly two months. He used sample stationery he purchased in London, bearing the address of their new home, which was under construction and would not be ready for occupancy until September 1874. The *City of Chester* was the Inman Line steamship that he had sailed on from New York in November 1873; its physician has not been identified.

A Miracle Cure (pages 103–4): Mark Twain's letter of 1 August 1883 to the Magnetic Rock Spring Company was published in the 11 August 1883 issue of the *Colfax (Iowa) Clipper*, from which this text is taken. Temperance was, in fact, "deeply imbedded" in Clemens's family. His brother was at least intermittently a teetotaler, and his mother and sister were temperance crusaders and members of the first chapter of the Woman's Christian Temperance Union. The cause did not take root in Clemens himself, however. In 1906 he recalled that in 1850 he joined the Hannibal chapter of the Cadets of Temperance, the youth adjunct of the local Sons of Temperance, which had been organized in 1847. He was drawn by the red sash that members wore on festive occasions, but the attraction, and his membership, lasted only three months.

Experience of the McWilliamses with Membranous Croup (pages 104–11): This text is taken from the American Publishing Company's 1875 first edition of *Mark Twain's Sketches, New and Old* (85–92). Clemens based the McWilliamses on himself and his wife, Olivia, although he borrowed the name from John and Esther McWilliams, newlyweds he befriended while living in Buffalo and editing the *Buffalo Express* in 1869, the year before his own marriage. John McWilliams was a bookkeeper in the Buffalo office of Olivia's family's coal firm.

Smoking, Diet, and Health at Age Seventy (pages 111–15): This excerpt from Clemens's 5 December 1905 speech is taken from the 1910 edition of *Mark Twain's Speeches* (427–32). Clemens made these remarks at the grand seventieth-birthday dinner given him at Delmonico's restaurant in New York City on 5 December 1905. The dinner was held on that date because his actual birthday, 30 November, was Thanksgiving Day that year. The host for the event (the "chairman" mentioned by Clemens in his speech) was Colonel George Harvey, president of Harper and Brothers. The guest list of 170 included some of Clemens's oldest friends and many of the leading literary lights of the day. It did not include Joseph H. Choate, the prominent lawyer and ambassador to Great Britain, to whom Clemens alluded in passing. One of the highlights of the evening was the reading of a letter of tribute from President Theodore Roosevelt. Clemens's father, John Marshall Clemens, a lawyer, storekeeper, and county court judge, died in March 1847, at the age of forty-eight. As to Clemens's rule "never to smoke when asleep," William Dean Howells offered some clarification in *My Mark Twain:* "He always went to bed with a cigar in his mouth, and sometimes, mindful of my fire insurance, I went up and took it away, still burning, after he had fallen asleep. I do not know how much a man may smoke and live, but apparently he smoked as much as a man could, for he smoked incessantly."

### 6. PARENTING AND THE ETHICAL CHILD

Illustration (page 116): The Clemens family on the veranda, or "ombra," as they called it (Italian for "shade"), of their Hartford house, photographed in 1884. *Left to right:* Clara, age ten; Samuel L. Clemens; Jean, age almost four; Olivia Clemens; and Susy, age twelve.

Maxims (page 118): "The most permanent lessons in morals" is from *A Tramp Abroad*, chapter 47. "It is a shameful thing to insult a little child" is from "Which Was the Dream?" (1897; first published in 1967).

The Late Benjamin Franklin (pages 119–22): This sketch first appeared in Mark Twain's monthly "Memoranda" column in the *Galaxy* magazine for July 1870 (10:138–40), from which this text is taken. Mark Twain's statement that Franklin was born "simultaneously in two different houses" is an exaggeration: he was born in 1706 in a modest house on Boston's Milk Street, and shortly afterward the family moved to Hanover Street, an address that some assumed to be his birthplace. His father was a tallow chandler and soap boiler, and young Benjamin's formal education was cut short when he was ten years old so that he might learn that trade. He invented his economical Pennsylvanian Fireplace, commonly known as the Franklin stove, in 1741. Franklin's suggestion that the army "go back to bows and arrows in place of bayonets and muskets" was contained in his letter of 11 February 1776 to General Charles Lee: "Those were good Weapons, not wisely laid aside," he wrote. Mark Twain quotes or freely misquotes five maxims that he ascribes to Franklin: the epigraph ("Never put off . . . just as well") skews Franklin's "Have you somewhat to do To-morrow, do it To-day" in Poor Richard's almanac for 1758; "A groat a day's a penny a year" recalls Franklin's "A Pin a day is a Groat a Year" from Poor Richard's almanac for 1737 as well as "six pounds a year is but a groat a day" in Franklin's "Advice to a Young Tradesman" (1748); "Procrastination is the thief of time" is actually from Edward Young's didactic poem *Night Thoughts* (1742–45); "Virtue is its own reward" is the common translation of a saying attributed to Cicero; Franklin's "early to bed" is from Poor Richard's almanac for 1758.

On Theft and Conscience (pages 122–23): This excerpt from Mark Twain's 4 June 1902 speech at the University of Missouri commencement exercises is taken from the 1910 edition of *Mark Twain's Speeches* (339–40).

On Training Children (pages 123–24): This excerpt is from the manuscript of "A Family Sketch," written in 1906, at the James S. Copley Library in La Jolla, California. Clara (1874–1962) was Clemens's second daughter.

A Sampling of Childish Ethics (pages 125–32): These anecdotes are extracted from the manuscript of "A Record of The Small Foolishnesses of Susie & 'Bay' Clemens (Infants.)," compiled between 1876 and 1885, which is at the Clifton Waller Barrett Library, University of Virginia. Here Clemens alludes to the "ombra," the veranda of his Hartford house, a favorite family spot for dining, relaxing, and entertaining; his children, Olivia Susan (1872–96, called "Susie" and "Susy"), Clara (1874–1962, called "Bay" from Susy's mispronunciation of "baby"), and Jane Lampton (1880–1909, called "Jean"); Elisabeth Gillette (Lilly) Warner, a close friend and neighbor, the wife of George H. Warner and the sister-in-law of Charles Dudley Warner; Clara Spaulding, of Elmira, New York, Olivia Clemens's lifelong friend; Susan L. Crane, Olivia's foster sister and aunt to the Clemens children; *Daniel Boone, the Pioneer of Kentucky* (1872), by John S. C. Abbott; and the Reverend Thomas K. Beecher, of Park Congregational Church in Elmira, friend and pastor to Olivia's family.

Youthful Misdemeanors (pages 133–34): This excerpt from Mark Twain's 28 November 1902 sixty-seventh birthday dinner speech at the Metropolitan Club in New York City is taken from the 1910 edition of *Mark Twain's Speeches* (369–71). John B. Briggs (1837–1907) was one of Clemens's closest boyhood friends. Clemens evidently depicted him as Ben Rogers in both *Tom Sawyer* and *Huckleberry Finn*.

Advice to Youth (pages 134–37): Mark Twain wrote this draft for a speech around 1882. The manuscript at the Mark Twain Papers, The Bancroft Library, supplies the text. The speech, with the title supplied by Albert Bigelow Paine, was published in the 1923 edition of *Mark Twain's Speeches* (104–8). The occasion for this speech has not been determined. The maxim "Truth is mighty and will prevail" is from the first book of the Apocrypha, 1 Esdras 4:41. The Boston "monument to the man who discovered anæsthesia" was the thirty-foot-high granite and marble Ether Monument, by sculptor J. Q. A. Ward, erected in 1868 near one corner of the Public Garden. It commemorated the demonstration of ether's effectiveness by physician and dentist William T. G. Morton, at Massachusetts General Hospital, in 1846. Three others had a claim to the discovery of anesthesia, however: Dr. Crawford W. Long, who used ether in Jefferson, Georgia, in 1842, a fact not generally known until after Morton's demonstration; Boston physician and geologist Charles T. Jackson, who suggested the use of ether to Morton in 1846; and Hartford dentist Horace Wells, Morton's teacher and for a time his partner, who as early as 1840 suggested nitrous oxide inhalation and as early as 1844 used it on himself and others. Clemens endorsed Wells's claim. Clemens recommended two much-reprinted religious works: Frederick William Robertson's *Sermons Preached at Trinity Chapel, Brighton* (first published in 1855), and Richard Baxter's *The Saint's Everlasting Rest; or, A Treatise of the Blessed State of the Saints in Their Enjoyment of God in Heaven* (first published in 1650).

## 7. CLOTHES, FASHION, AND STYLE

Illustration (page 138): The bare-chested portrait was probably taken in 1884, when Mark Twain was forty-eight years old, in order to serve as a reference photograph for the young sculptor Karl Gerhardt, whose art studies in Paris Mark Twain had financed. In the summer of 1884, Gerhardt sculpted a clay bust of his mentor that he later cast in plaster and bronze. Mark Twain was so pleased with the result that he decided to use a photograph of the plaster version as a frontispiece for *Huckleberry Finn*, which was published in February 1885.

Maxims (page 140): "Be careless in your dress if you must, but keep a tidy soul" is from "Pudd'nhead Wilson's New Calendar" in *Following the Equator*, chapter 23. "Clothes make the man" is from *More Maxims of Mark* (6).

A Fashion Item (pages 141–42): This piece was first published as part of Mark Twain's letter of 31 January 1868 to the *Chicago Republican*, 8 February 1868 (2), from which this text is drawn. In 1872 Mark Twain republished it under the title "Fashion Item" in *Mark Twain's Sketches* (London: George Routledge and Sons) and in 1874 as "A Fashion Item" in *The Choice Humorous Works of Mark Twain* (London: Chatto and Windus), from which the title is drawn. General Ulysses S. Grant and his wife, Julia, held a reception in Washington for members of Congress and the general public on the evening of 15 January 1868.

The Hand of Fashion (pages 143–49): This excerpt from chapter 7 of *The Innocents Abroad* is reprinted from the American Publishing Company's 1869 first edition (73–75). The cast of *Quaker City* excursion characters here includes, in addition to Mark Twain and Dan Slote: former Confederate Colonel William Ritenour Denny, of Winchester, Virginia; and William Gibson, a Jamestown, Pennsylvania, physician who had been commissioned by the United States Department of Agriculture and by the Smithsonian Institution to gather specimens and mementos. The *Quaker City* surgeon and the passengers who were the prototypes for "the General," "the Judge," and "the Commodore" have not been identified.

That White Suit (pages 149–50): This extract is from an interview with Mark Twain in Washington, D.C., on 7 December 1906, "Mark Twain in White Amuses Congressmen," published in the *New York Times* the following day (2). Clemens saw his "best-dressed man" in Hawaii (the Sandwich Islands) in 1866, while there as a travel correspondent for the *Sacramento Union*.

Clothes and Deception (pages 150–52): This excerpt from chapter 37 of *Following the Equator* is reprinted from the American Publishing Company's 1897 first edition (340–44). Clemens describes the clothing worn in Colombo, the capital of Ceylon (now Sri Lanka), one of the stops on his 1895–96 world lecture tour. The Galle Face was a grassy esplanade fronting on the Indian Ocean. *Galle* derives from *galla*, Sinhalese for "rock."

A Sumptuous Robe (page 153): This excerpt from Mark Twain's 11 January 1908 speech to the Lotos Club of New York is taken from its 1911 publication in *After Dinner Speeches at the Lotos Club* (344–55), under the title "Samuel L. Clemens at the Dinner in His Honor." Clemens had belonged to the Lotos Club since 1873. The club had been founded in 1870 to bring together journalists, authors, artists, actors, musicians, and interested members of the business community. The "giddy costume" was the gown Clemens first wore on 26 June 1907, when Oxford University conferred upon him an honorary doctor of letters degree. It is now on display at the Mark Twain Museum in Hannibal, Missouri.

## 8. IN CASE OF EMERGENCY

Illustration (page 154): Mark Twain was photographed, wet and disheveled after a swim, on 10 April 1908 on the grounds of Bay House, the residence of William H. Allen, the United States vice-consul in Hamilton, Bermuda. The photograph was taken by Mark Twain's secretary, Isabel V. Lyon.

Maxims (page 156): "The proverb says" is from an autobiographical dictation of 23 January 1907 at the Mark Twain Papers, The Bancroft Library. "We should be careful" is from "Pudd'nhead Wilson's New Calendar" in *Following the Equator*, chapter 11.

Playing "Bear" (pages 157–60): This excerpt is taken from Mark Twain's autobiographical manuscript of 1900, "Scraps from My Autobiography," at the Mark Twain Papers, The Bancroft Library, as revised by Mark Twain and published in the 21 September 1906 *North American Review* (183:453–56). The Clemens family, in Hannibal since 1839, moved into the small frame house at 206 Hill Street in 1844. It is now preserved as the Mark Twain Boyhood Home. In 1849, when she gave the party Clemens remembers, Pamela Clemens was twenty-two years old. Sandy was a young slave who worked for, but was not owned by, the Clemens family in Hannibal. The witness to Clemens's nude gyrations whom he here calls "Mary Wilson, because that was not her name," was Sarah H. Robards (1836–1918), a classmate of his and a piano student of Pamela's. In his autobiographical writings,

Clemens frequently gave fictitious names to the people he discussed. He did not intend their real names to be known until that information could no longer threaten their privacy or that of their descendants.

An Apparition (pages 161–62): This excerpt from chapter 18 of *The Innocents Abroad* is reprinted from the American Publishing Company's 1869 first edition (175–77). Clemens told a somewhat different version of this story in his 7 March 1906 speech at Barnard College in New York City. He explained then that the dead man was a stranger who had been stabbed while passing through Hannibal. Clemens's father, John Marshall Clemens, in his capacity of justice of the peace, took charge of the corpse.

The Great Earthquake in San Francisco (pages 162–70): The text of this excerpt from Mark Twain's October 1865 letter to the *New York Weekly Review* is taken from the Mark Twain Project's 1981 *Early Tales & Sketches, Volume 2* (303–10). The earthquake Clemens describes occurred on 8 October 1865. He alludes to *The Greek Slave*, Hiram Powers's sculpture of a female nude, a sensation at the London Crystal Palace exposition in 1851; Brobdingnag, the land of giants in Jonathan Swift's *Gulliver's Travels;* Thomas H. Selby and Company's manufactory of shot, bullets, and sheet and bar lead, an octagonal tower 180 feet tall at the corner of First and Howard Streets; the Reverend S. S. Harmon, of the Female College of the Pacific in Oakland, which had been the subject of talk in September 1865, when two of its students were involved in a sexual escapade with a prominent pianist; and Horatio Stebbins, pastor of the Geary Street First Unitarian Church, formerly presided over by the Reverend Thomas Starr King.

Escape of the Tarantulas (pages 170–72): This extract from chapter 21 of *Roughing It* is reprinted from the Mark Twain Project's 1993 edition (144–46). Clemens here gives an account of the terror that resulted when his Nevada friend Robert M. Howland ("Bob H———") accidentally loosed the collection of spiders belonging to another resident of the Carson City boardinghouse kept by Mrs. Margret Murphy ("Mrs. O'Flannigan"). The "zephyr" was the legendary Nevada wind, much exaggerated for comic effect by local journalists.

Burglary and the Well-Tempered Householder (pages 173–76): This excerpt is taken from the autobiographical dictation of 8 February 1906 at the Mark Twain Papers, The Bancroft Library, as revised by Mark Twain and published in the 19 October 1906 *North American Review* (183:713–15). In 1885, when she was thirteen, Susy Clemens began a biography of her father. More than twenty years later, he included numerous excerpts from it in his autobiographical dictations. In the passage that Clemens quoted in this dictation, Susy remarked that "our burglar alarm is often out of order" and described some of his frustration in trying to make it function. In an 1882 sketch, "The McWilliamses and the Burglar Alarm," Clemens had himself turned his difficulties with the alarm to humorous account.

Under a Policeman's Eye (pages 176–82): This excerpt is taken from Mark Twain's unfinished manuscript "The Innocents Adrift," written between 1891 and 1893, which is at the Mark Twain Papers, The Bancroft Library. It was published for the first time by Albert Bigelow Paine as "Down the Rhône" in the 1923 *Europe and Elsewhere* (129–68). In his manuscript Clemens gave himself four fictional travel companions, in addition to a courier and a boatman. The overcoat incident occurred in February 1882, just after the burglary in which Clemens lost his own overcoat. He was in New York to attend the fifteenth annual exhibition of the American Water-Color Society, at the National Academy of Design. The acquaintance whose overcoat Clemens borrowed was Francis Hopkinson Smith, author, engineer, and painter.

# Works Cited

Clemens, Samuel L. (Mark Twain)

1869. *The Innocents Abroad; or, The New Pilgrims' Progress.* Hartford: American Publishing Company.

1870–1909. Autobiographical Writings and Autobiographical Dictations. Beginning in 1870 and continuing sporadically over the next decades, Mark Twain wrote—and occasionally dictated—a number of autobiographical essays, primarily about his family history and his business affairs. These he pigeonholed. Finally, in 1906, he began his autobiography in earnest, dictating to a secretary who typed each day's installment. He hoped to create a uniquely honest form of memoir, conversational and organic, broaching topics as they occurred to him. Although he edited and published parts of the autobiography in the *North American Review* in twenty-five installments in 1906 and 1907 (collected and republished by Michael J. Kiskis in 1990), he intended the bulk of his memoir—encompassing both the manuscript and the dictated portions—to be published posthumously. The hundreds of typescript pages that resulted from his dictations between 1906 and 1909, organized by date in more than 250 folders, are in the Mark Twain Papers of The Bancroft Library. After Mark Twain's death, selections from the autobiographical writings were published piecemeal in periodicals and in editions by Albert Bigelow Paine in 1924, Bernard DeVoto in 1940, and Charles Neider in 1959.

1872. *Mark Twain's Sketches.* Selected and revised by the author. Copyright edition. London: George Routledge and Sons.

1872. *Roughing It.* Hartford: American Publishing Company.

1873. *The Gilded Age: A Tale of To-day.* Charles Dudley Warner, coauthor. Hartford: American Publishing Company.

1874. *The Choice Humorous Works of Mark Twain.* Revised and corrected by the author. London: Chatto and Windus.

1875. *Mark Twain's Sketches, New and Old*. Hartford: American Publishing Company.

1880. *A Tramp Abroad*. Hartford: American Publishing Company.

1882. *The Stolen White Elephant, Etc.* Boston: James R. Osgood and Co.

1885. *Adventures of Huckleberry Finn*. New York: Charles L. Webster and Co.

1894. *The Tragedy of Pudd'nhead Wilson and the Comedy Those Extraordinary Twins*. Hartford: American Publishing Company.

1897. *Following the Equator: A Journey around the World*. Hartford: American Publishing Company.

1897–98. "My Autobiography. [Random Extracts from it.]" Manuscript of seventy-five pages at the Mark Twain Papers, The Bancroft Library. Published, with omissions, as "Early Days" in *Mark Twain's Autobiography* (1924).

1900. "Scraps from My Autobiography. Playing 'Bear.' Herrings. Jim Wolf and the Cats." Manuscript of forty-two pages at the Mark Twain Papers, The Bancroft Library. Published in *Mark Twain's Autobiography* (1924).

1906. "A Family Sketch." Manuscript of sixty-five pages. James S. Copley Library, La Jolla, California.

1910. *Mark Twain's Speeches*. Edited by Albert Bigelow Paine. With an introduction by William Dean Howells. New York: Harper and Brothers.

1923. *Europe and Elsewhere*. Edited by Albert Bigelow Paine. With an appreciation by Brander Matthews and an introduction by Albert Bigelow Paine. New York: Harper and Brothers.

1923. *Mark Twain's Speeches*. Edited by Albert Bigelow Paine. With an introduction by Albert Bigelow Paine and an appreciation by William Dean Howells. New York: Harper and Brothers.

1924. *Mark Twain's Autobiography*. Edited by Albert Bigelow Paine. 2 vols. New York: Harper and Brothers.

1927. *More Maxims of Mark*. Edited by Merle Johnson. New York: Privately printed.

1940. *Mark Twain in Eruption*. Edited by Bernard DeVoto. New York: Harper and Brothers.

1959. *The Autobiography of Mark Twain*. Edited by Charles Neider. New York: Harper and Brothers.

1967. *Mark Twain's Which Was the Dream? and Other Symbolic Writings of the Later Years*. Edited by John S. Tuckey. Berkeley, Los Angeles, and London: University of California Press.

1972. *Mark Twain's Fables of Man*. Edited by John S. Tuckey. Berkeley, Los Angeles, and London: University of California Press.

1979. *Early Tales & Sketches, Volume 1 (1851–1864)*. Edited by Edgar Marquess Branch and Robert H. Hirst, with the assistance of Harriet Elinor Smith. The Works of Mark Twain. Berkeley, Los Angeles, and London: University of California Press.

1981. *Early Tales & Sketches, Volume 2 (1864–1865)*. Edited by Edgar Marquess Branch and Robert H. Hirst, with the assistance of Harriet Elinor Smith. The Works of Mark Twain. Berkeley, Los Angeles, and London: University of California Press.

1990. *Mark Twain's Own Autobiography: The Chapters from the "North American Review."* With an introduction and notes by Michael J. Kiskis. Madison: University of Wisconsin Press.

1993. *Roughing It*. Edited by Harriet Elinor Smith, Edgar Marquess Branch, Lin Salamo, and Robert Pack Browning. The Works of Mark Twain. Berkeley, Los Angeles, and London: University of California Press.

1997. *Mark Twain's Letters, Volume 5: 1872–1873*. Edited by Lin Salamo and Harriet Elinor Smith. The Mark Twain Papers. Berkeley, Los Angeles, and London: University of California Press.

2002. *Mark Twain's Letters, Volume 6: 1874–1875*. Edited by Michael B. Frank and Harriet Elinor Smith. The Mark Twain Papers. Berkeley, Los Angeles, and London: University of California Press.

2003. *Adventures of Huckleberry Finn*. Edited by Victor Fischer and Lin Salamo. The Works of Mark Twain. Berkeley, Los Angeles, and London: University of California Press.

Elderkin, John, Chester S. Lord, and Charles W. Price, eds. 1911. *After Dinner Speeches at the Lotos Club*. New York: Lotos Club.

Howells, William Dean. 1910. *My Mark Twain: Reminiscences and Criticisms*. New York: Harper and Brothers.

Lawton, Mary. 1925. *A Lifetime with Mark Twain: The Memories of Katy Leary, for Thirty Years His Faithful and Devoted Servant*. New York: Harcourt, Brace and Co.

Paine, Albert Bigelow. 1912. *Mark Twain: A Biography*. 3 vols. New York: Harper and Brothers.

# ⚜ Acknowledgments ⚜

The selection and annotation of the texts in this volume have depended on the extraordinary files of original materials and collateral documents gathered over several decades by the editorial staff at the Mark Twain Project. The editors of this volume wish to acknowledge this cumulative debt, as well as the leadership and guidance of Robert H. Hirst, the General Editor of the Mark Twain Project since 1980. We thank our editorial colleague Harriet Elinor Smith for assistance on textual matters and Michael R. Ferguson, a graduate student researcher at the Project, for help with proofreading. Professor Robert Middlekauff graciously shared his historical expertise, and Kevin Mac Donnell made available to us a little-known photograph. Dan Johnston, head of the Digital Imaging Lab at the Library at the University of California, Berkeley, and his staff photographers Jiro Marubayashi and Sarah Grew provided us with fine digital images of rare materials.

Our many talented colleagues at the University of California Press—including Susan Ecklund, Stephanie Rubin, and our production coordinator, Sam Rosenthal—have smoothed our road through production and publication. The road map for that process has been in the capable hands of our sponsoring editor at the Press, Laura Cerruti, our project editor, Laura Harger, and the book's designer, Nicole Hayward: their timely suggestions we gratefully acknowledge.

L.S.    V.F.    M.B.F.

TEXT: 11/14 Fournier — DISPLAY: Hamilton Light — DESIGNER: Nicole Hayward
COMPOSITOR: BookMatters, Berkeley — PRINTER & BINDER: Edwards Brothers, Inc.